Published by Golden Foothills Press
1443 E. Washington Boulevard, #232
Pasadena, CA 91104
www.GoldenFoothillsPress.com

ISBN 978-0-9969632-4-4

Cover photo: "Tree Silhouette with Roots." ID: 38425831, www.shutterstock.com.
     Modified by continuing its color bands to a full bleed around book cover.
Book design: Thelma T. Reyna
Cover design: Thelma T. Reyna, Victor Cass, & Dom Gilormini
Printed in the United States of America

First Edition: 2018

Altadena Poetry Review

Anthology 2018

Edited by

Pauline Dutton
Elline Lipkin

Golden Foothills PRESS

ANTHOLOGY SELECTION COMMITTEE

For the fourth year in a row, the following local distinguished poets served as committee members working closely with the Poet Laureate of Altadena (CA) Library District to choose poetry for publication in the *Altadena Poetry Review Anthology.* These poets assisted current Poet Laureate Elline Lipkin, and her co-editor Pauli Dutton, in doing this vital curatorial work for the 2018 edition of this book. (New to the committee this year were Mary and Cathie.)

Tim Callahan
Gloriana Casey
Mary Fitzpatrick
Gerda Govine Ituarte
Briony James
Cathie Sandstrom
Elsa M. J. Seifert

INTRODUCTION

The Altadena Poetry Review was birthed in 2003 as the Altadena Public Library's *Poetry and Cookies* anthology and reading event. Its purpose was to serve as a community project to provide new poets from Altadena and the surrounding communities an opportunity to have their work published and to read their poetry in public.

Three years ago, when I was about to retire as Principal Librarian at Altadena Library, I asked the newly inaugurated library Poet Laureate, Thelma T. Reyna, if she would head a committee to continue the tradition of the annual anthology. Fortunately, Thelma agreed, and with her experience as professional editor and owner of Golden Foothills Press, she gave the book a stunning makeover, including re-naming it the *Altadena Poetry Review* (APR). This title signifies its increased professionalism as a peer-reviewed publication and reputable literary journal that goes beyond local boundaries. The poets published in the APR represent the best of both worlds, reaching out to a wide area of well-regarded poets for publication consideration and including excellent local talent, many of them having built a reputation that straddles the local scene and the literary world beyond. This approach has garnered the APR both local and national awards.

To insure the continuation of the *Altadena Poetry Review*, this year the editors reluctantly asked for a submission fee while at the same time offered several scholarships as well. We fervently hoped that the fee would not discourage anyone from contributing nor affect the publication's high level of content. Although there were some who chose not to submit due to fees, we attracted many new poets and ended up with close to 300 (297) submissions, and 106 poets are being published in this anthology.

Although the fee would help pay for a book for each of the published poets, as the increased costs of this year's publication loomed ahead, again Library Director Mindy Kittay encouraged Elline to ask the Friends of the Library for help. The organization enthusiastically replied in the form of a substantial donation to cover these costs.

For all of this and more, we would like to express our overwhelming gratitude for the support, both emotional and financial, of Altadena Library Director, Mindy Kittay, and the Friends of the Altadena Library. Without their assistance, this project would not have been able to continue. They well live up to the quote noted on the Friends of the Library homepage: "The word 'Friend' immediately brings to mind the people who help celebrate all the goodness in life and stand steadfast when times are troubled, who offer support when it's needed and offer counsel to help us see the straight path. We count on our friends and they count on us."

I am also very grateful to our Poet Laureate Elline Lipkin for her many contributions as co-editor, for organizing and running the committee, and for her keen poetic sense on how to best present a poet's work. We are also grateful to Thelma, who agreed to again take the reins as publisher this year, which will allow for a stable publishing presence.

In addition, we thank our fine Selection Committee for their hours of reading, consideration, and refinement of many of the poems seen here. the Anthology Selection Committee, all volunteers, includes Tim Callahan, Gloriana Casey, Gerda Govine Ituarte, Briony James, Elsa M. J. Seifert, Mary Fitzpatrick, and Cathie Sandstrom. We also thank the extraordinary poets who sent their work to us. Many times, I cried as I came across a particularly beautiful phrase and felt deep gratitude to be part of this inspiring process. Still, after a total of 16 years of working on the *Poetry and Cookies* project and the *Altadena Poetry Review*, I have decided it is time for me to retire from the APR. With the library's promise of continued support, the institution of a fee to help with rising publishing costs, and Thelma continuing as publisher, I can now fathom the APR as able to continue without me and trust the future of this publication to the library's new Poet Laureate and new editor/co-editor.

My deep gratitude to all who have assisted with this publication, to you readers, and to the poets whose work of surprising humor, beauty, and insight lies within these pages.

--Pauli Dutton
Co-Editor, *Altadena Poetry Review* 2017 and 2018
Founder, *Poetry and Cookies (P&C) Anthology*
Founder of P&C Public Reading Event
Altadena Public Library: Principal Librarian, 1985-2014
Friends of the Library Liaison
Poet

FOREWORD
From the Poet Laureate

"Poets are the unacknowledged legislators of the world" wrote Percy Bysshe Shelley in his *Defence of Poetry*, published in 1821. Almost two centuries later, I like to think that understanding how the power of words and the magic of language can produce such lyrical effects is still as strong as ever. And I am grateful to see that there is acknowledgment of its importance in our daily lives. During the past two years it has been my pleasure and honor to be acknowledged as Altadena's Poet Laureate. I have been humbled by the collective talent and passion for poetry found within our community.

This past March I flew to Tampa, FL to attend The Associated Writing Program conference, which brings together over 10,000 attendees who all love the literary arts. I spoke on a panel entitled, "Literary Public Citizen: The Laureate in the Community," which had representatives from different corners of the country, yet all of us shared the same mission: to bring the joy of poetry to our communities. I was proud to hold up a copy of the *Altadena Poetry Review* and to speak about my excitement about this year's issue. I also spoke about our community-wide tradition of the annual "Poetry & Cookies Reading Event," and there was amazement at how many poets come out to participate each year.

Making poetry an essential part of our beautiful community has been deeply meaningful to me, and it will be bittersweet to step down from this role. Knowing that these traditions, so well beloved, will continue is a solace. My enormous and eternal gratitude to Pauli Dutton, whose vision of bringing poetry to Altadena has made a tremendous difference in the lives of so many. Her work on this issue has been nothing short of untiring, amazing, and inspiring. As well, huge bouquets of gratitude to Thelma T. Reyna, whose community vision is endless, and the addition of her wonderful local press, Golden Foothills, will only increase the literary gains we can then share. Feeling part of a team in my laureateship has made all the difference and seems at the heart of what cultivating literary citizenship is about.

My great thanks to the Altadena Poetry Review Selection Committee who worked so hard on this issue. None of this could have happened without their diligent work. Our collective gratitude goes to the

Altadena Public Library itself and the network of amazing people who keep it at the hub of our community's life. Its director, Mindy Kittay, has been our generous supporter, as have been the Friends of the Library, whose help was crucial in getting this year's edition out. My thanks as well to *Poets & Writers* for their grants, which helped to sponsor two programs during this past year through the funding it has received from the James Irvine Foundation and the Hearst Foundation. Poet Genevieve Kaplan taught a workshop entitled "Crafting a Poem, Crafting a Book" last fall, and poet Felicia Montes taught a workshop based on the connection between poetry and healing this spring.

It has been a collective effort of so many to bring this year's anthology to fruition, and I am thrilled with this beautiful edition. May it bring the pleasure and power of poetry home for you — home in our community of Altadena. As we welcome the next Poet Laureate soon, I hope the connections made during these past two years will continue to flourish as we all bring forward the poems we need to write.

--Elline Lipkin, Ph.D.
Poet Laureate, Altadena Library District, 2016-2018
Co-Editor, *Altadena Poetry Review 2017* and 2018

TABLE OF CONTENTS

Author Biographies, 215-235

I AM

I touched the mirror, and
it was flat and cold.
But my reflection was me,
so I must be real.

I looked into the eyes that
were black and cold and
I couldn't see my soul,
But I must be real.

It mattered little what I
thought. Without a voice
I was unheard.
Yet, I must be real.

I touched the mirror and
pulled the nightmare
from behind the veil and
screamed, "I am real."

And the mirror…the mirror shattered.

--Chris Anak

Originally published in *The Courage to Write,* 2011

ON A SONNET'S PROCESS

this is more about a feeling than a message. this is sculpted, structured with
great obsession, but it's free-flowing as bebop. this is the rage of every
awful memory, like a hot coal in a fist, but: still, like a stallion at rest.
this is the curve of sound and seawaves, like canyon walls eroded
by wind and time. this not a scream but, rather: an evocation of
an orgasm.
see how each word's a molecule, crashing, creating reactions: see how
they are volatile, medicinal, depending on how they combine. see
them in their alliterative phrases, subsonic consonants, a pattern
of ants and stars. see this strictly on this page, then hear it in
your solitude: feel the reverb in your guts: allow nothing to
distract you.
this is not spoken word: this is much louder in its silence.
this is no lecture. this is bewitchment: a speechless kiss.

--Allan Aquino

BIG BROTHER

With nowhere to go
And seeking relief
I suddenly heard
A hum above me
I looked to the sky
And hovering above
I saw a drone
Observing me

Caught in midstream
Awakened what seemed
A moment serene
While the plane bore down
To see me there
With the cockpit open
Suspended in air

It's a wicked world
This day and age
Orwellian
The playing field's changed
You can lock your doors
You can pull the shades
But they'll find you out
You cannot escape

And then I looked up
At an ominous sky
At an alien craft
That emerged from on high
Then swooped down
And gobbled the drone
It turned around
And headed for home

--Richard Ash

WHAT'S HAPPENED TO YOUTH

What's Happened to Youth
It's gone to yesterday
Once ensconced in a baseball glove
The ball has gone astray
Deep into the forest
Where it cannot be found
A remnant of a bygone day
Buried beneath the ground

What's Happened to Youth
I'd run across the yard
In hot pursuit of fire flies
I'd capture in a jar
But time you cannot conceal
Imprison or delay
Like snowflakes in the winter
In spring they melt away

Glory to the moments
Though they never come again
And all the days of youth
Never thought to end
Glory to the seasons
And all the years of yore
For memories I'll be grateful
Forevermore

What's Happened to Youth
I didn't see it leave
It rolled across a sandy shore
And then rolled out to sea
Gone without a warning

Gone without a sign
Like ever-changing rhythms
The ebb and flow of time

--Richard Ash

THIS TABLE

Mom I have your table
Centering my life on it like you did
Visions of you late at night at this table
Your adding machine busy calculating
The bookkeeping for the family store
After dinner was cleared away
My brothers and I in bed
You put on your accounting hat
Do you see me on my computer late at night
paying bills on this table?

Hundreds of miles away and decades ago
So many people gathered at this table
To celebrate birthdays, graduations, holidays
With the traditional dessert passing of a See's Candy Box
Circulating the long oval table until it was finished
Relatives always photographed
Smiling around this table

Routine nightly dinners at this table
The TV blaring news from the Viet Nam War
Hard to stomach those meals when President Johnson
Started his message
"My Fellow Americans,
Tonight I come to you with a heavy heart"
Knots in my stomach with 3 brothers of draft age

Do you see the people who enjoy this table now?
Do you see the tradition of long-stemmed candles lit for visitors?
Do you see me welcoming our relatives from across the pond to this table?
I hope so
I see you at this table

--Beth Baird

WAKE UP

She sits by the window
staring at the emerald bay
Wondering when he will return
She imagines him appearing over the grassy knoll
Running to her through the meadow
She imagines herself running toward him
Her heart skipping beats as they draw near

She looks up
Sounds of a car approaching
She turns her head from sea to road
The dream is broken
He is carried out of a van
 and placed in a wheelchair

--Beth Baird

UGLY SHOES

My flat feet beg
For ugly shoes
Not for fashion shown
On the news
They want to carry
My considerable weight
Enabling me to walk
With a steady gait
You'll never see me wearing
High heels
I simply don't like the way
That they feel
Those fancy shoes that they make in Rome
Won't find a way to my closet or home
So give me a pair of oxfords or flats,
Sneakers or loafers but nothing with spats
There are places to go that I want to see
I'm counting on ugly shoes to carry me.

--Kathee Bautista

BEAUTIFUL CHERRY

she was once fruitful
branching out in many ways
a cherry blossom
of impeccable beauty
who lives in our memories

--Ruth Blue

THREATENED SELF

If the needs, respect, future of all considered
were considered
the decision would be simple,
but it is not a decision that can be made
with ease

the words must be spoken with a calmness,
an aloofness
and with an abundance of adoration
if this is not the case
then the case will continue

to meet the needs, respect and future
of the one that decides
those left behind to deal with
the deal, the chaos
must learn
to prioritize
and
bend to power.

--Jack G Bowman

WINGS ON YOUR WHEELCHAIR

The wings on your wheelchair
Flutter through the waterfall of despair.
It lands softly, spokes gleaming
In a place where wounded boys will never die.

The braces on your legs
Are softly calling your name.
They feel neglected; as discarded
As your need to walk the earth you left.

The ropes and pulleys on your bed
Lay lifeless, gathering dust,
As spiders spin and dangle
Wondering where you are.

The flowers on your grave
Stand wilted, bent in admiration
For the crippled boy who wanders free,
Enslaved by steel and wheel no more.

--G. Larry Butler

Originally published in the author's *Here Lies Madness,* 2009.

I NEVER SAW HER AGAIN AFTER THE IGUANA

in memory of Thérèse

I didn't visit anymore.
I couldn't sleep on her floor
eye level with it—
I'd heard how she'd house-trained
how it would pad
to the shower to poop
how she kissed its cheeks
cradled it like a baby
and when it died
on that floor in Astoria
how she cried
and laid it out in state.
How she found it rigor mortised
like a stick the next morning
and how she wrapped that lizard lovingly
in layers of yesterdays' papers
bundled it in bag upon bag
and smuggled it onto the train
to take it into the park
for the final interment of *Iggy*.
　　　　But how impossible
burial became that day
with no shovel to dig
through rocks and hard dirt
and how she finally said goodbye
in the self-appointed role
of a priestess for reptilians
at a man-made lake
in the cathedral of Central Park.
How she propellered that plastic
like an incensed thurible lasso
of some holy rodeo pope. How
she arced it high as she let it go

to watch it soar
then splash and sink.
But only slightly
and not enough—
and how then it rose
absurdly again—
Just like Jesus.
Just like grief.
Hers then,   mine now.
Just like that.

--Thom Cagle

THE CASE OF THE PILLOW

What we have is not a sham
and I'm more than just fluff
or some cheap perch
for the curve of another's neck.
I've stuck with you
through fevers, flu
and soaked up tears
the friends grew tired of catching.
A sound guard to your heart-
broken bellows, I crook
to give comfort
to fill your arms when you're alone
and smother the alarm
on hungover dawns.
You pull no punches with profanity
night upon over-tossed night
until the calm comes in
and warm drool proves
you entrust me
as the cradle for your dreams.

--Thom Cagle

4-14-15 APRICOT MOON, BLOOD ECLIPSE
dedicated to the Gabrielino indigenous

orange mars shimmering earth shadows
moon milky full fresh beaming pied sunsets
gray-furred fingers sprinkling dark magic dust
unseen hands lifting curtain
majestic crimson buffalo radiant
grazing on golden light
luna de sangre
flows deep down mountains
native peoples rising from oceans

--Morgan Zo Callahan

THAW TO LIGHT

snow softening
firs greening
black morning birds
suddenly singing spring

--Morgan Zo Callahan

ABYSSES OF MAKING AND UNMAKING

High above us in the heavens
far below us in the sea
restless currents ever flowing
churn the waters and the sky
twin voids of new creation
without substance, undefined,
full of twisting turning torsion
and of making and unmaking
full of unrealized potential.

And in the heavens now are forming
sculpted lenses so serene.
Yet in their seeming silent stillness
they are shaped by constant motion,
and their crystalline-like structure
dissolves when currents cease to flow.
And blue sky, seeming calm,
is so full of turning fury
as ever mixing as the ocean.
Sky and sea are twin abysses
of creating and undoing.

Without effort on the thermals,
a soaring hawk now utters
a long drawn-out and desolate cry.
Then it sheds its rising thermal,
folds its wings and, like a missile,
full of fatal fury falling
dives upon its hapless prey.
And in the sea a shark is swimming,
swift and streamlined, lovely, deadly
agent of the sea's unmaking.

Hawks and sharks of fatal beauty
filled with fierce and furious joy
high above us and below us

ride the currents ever streaming
ever making and unmaking
in the forming and dissolving
ever flowing, ever churning
ever restless twin abysses,
voids of death and of creation.

--Tim Callahan

THAT PERFECT MOMENT

Viewing the cherry blossoms in the light
 of a silver moon, low and full, the lovers
were so taken by their exquisite beauty
they felt no moment could be so fair,
and so resolved to take their own lives
rather than exist beyond its perfection.

Just then a raven cawed, its raucous cry
spoiling the elegance of the moment.
Chagrined at its loss, the lovers resolved
to continue living until they might
someday recapture that instant
of sublime purity.

Alas! They never found it again.
And so endured a less than
perfect love for many years,
even into old age.

I heard this tale from their daughter.
They named her Raven.

--Tim Callahan

PILGRIM'S PROGRESS

With Live Oak tree branch staff
I keep balance as I hike
upon white and ashen gray boulders
of Eaton Canyon Wash.

Under white concrete bridge on Mount Wilson
Toll Road, I begin quest.
In less than hour walking along and across ankle
deep canyon creek, I complete half-mile trek.

The forty-foot waterfall tumbles into a wide pool
I know unless I wade into its waist deep, chilly
waters and stand under the falls, I am only
a spectator, not a participant.

Eaton Canyon Falls plummets my body.
I am baptized.
Water is sacred.
MNI WICONI!

When I wake up next morning, I am
a gray cloud covering Mount Wilson
and adjacent mountains along with
all the San Gabriel Valley cities.

Above me I view, as Edwin Hubble did for
the first time from his 100-inch Mount Wilson
telescope, billions of other galaxies
outside our tiny Milky Way home.

Below me, I conceal
cloudy vision to all people living
on plains who've yet
to be baptized.

--CaLokie (Carl Stilwell)

A NEOLIBERAL PASTORAL

The Market is my mantra
I want it all

He maketh me spray pesticides on green pastures
and leadeth me to build factories beside still waters
where I may lay its wastes

He guideth me to lay off union workers in my country
and move operations overseas to hire cheap labor
for the sake of maximizing profits

Yea, though I walk through a valley desertified by global warming,
I will fear no evil for my government is thy executive committee
Thy media and church, they comfort me

Thou preparest a banquet table of more than I could possibly eat
far from the sight of nearly a billion chronically undernourished people
Thou anointest beaches from Alaska to the Gulf of Mexico with oil spills

The landfills runneth over with planned obsolescent products
and electronic waste while garbage patches swirl in the oceans
with non-biodegradable plastic bags and single use styrofoam cups

Surely wealth and power shall follow me all the days of my life
and exponential economic growth will continue world without end
on a planet of finite resources
Amen   Amen

--CaLokie (Carl Stilwell)

MY OBJECT LIFE

my street is usually quiet...sometimes it can't control itself

my apartment ain't getting any younger...just ask the walls, the sofa, the carpet, the drapes

my TV's feeling neglected (if it wasn't for the Lakers)

my clothes are a little concerned about belly weight

my car wants to believe I can continue to maintain her; I see her interior roof start to fray

my CD's wish I would still be faithful to them; lately I've been driving with MP3's

my cell phone doesn't like me to receive calls from the wrong poet, if you know who I mean

my wallet and refrigerator are OK, both could use the insertion of some lettuce, instead of the constant taking out of plastic

my computer's very happy; we touch each other every day

the microwave wonders when life will be cleaner

the clock knows I'd rather not look in the mirror

the bed remembers better nights

the tissue box worries though if I'll ever cry again

--Don Kingfisher Campbell

PLANET OF THE OREOS

so delightful this black oceaned and white continented world

the round black framed white bellied people enjoy eating

black crusted pizza covered with creamy white topping

as they sit at their white table-clothed black tables and

wear black and white dresses and suits and ties simply to

exit their white windowed black houses and walk on

white stone walkways around black bladed grass to go in

to their black cars sporting white rims which roll down

black (white lines through the middle) highway arrive at

circular black concrete plaza and lounge on raised white platform

dark and light mouths open in delight at the joy of living

on a delicious planet with black sky and white clouds except

for the fact their teeth are white with black spots all over

which they try to clean by taking milk river baths while

standing on black stones as the white sun shines in the night

--Don Kingfisher Campbell

A FLEETING LINE

Lying in bed
flannel sheets cozy
lights still on
a line across my mind
what was it

Why didn't I remember to
have that pen and paper handy
what was that scene, phrase, image
if I got out of bed
I might lose that string of words forever

Maybe it answered the letter he sent
maybe it was dialogue
she needed to say in a
special way to him
or to herself

Please recapture it
play it back so I can hear the
melody those words played
maybe I'll test fate and get up

to find that pen and paper
but is the risk too great
will the devil in the words
whisk them away forever

Maybe I can get up so quietly
that my second self
won't realize I'm gone
and while this second self
listens for the footsteps of

that whispering phrase
I can search for a working
pen and scrap of paper
to capture
that elusive thought once again

--Christine Candland

FORGOTTEN

The door opened and closed
the floor boards squeaked
and told stories that
held the house together for years.

The door opened again
she didn't get out
but stayed inside and became
part of the woodwork and
the floors that squeaked

Outside the window
the cottonwoods sang
to the muses who sat on the large
boulder invisible to everyone
but the most curious

--Christine Candland

PERSEPHONE & DEMETER

a police escort led me from my mother's womb.
the umbilical cord around my neck
couldn't keep me silent for long.
i was raised with strength, guidance,
the perseverance of a rumbling storm.
"do not let them see you cry.
you cry in the shower, your pillow,
my arms, but to them you raise that chin high."
my mother did not plant a flower,
but a tree with feet rooted to Gaea,
eyes like soil, and a laugh like the wind.
my mother is the sun,
and i rise to meet her.

--Julissa Marie Cárdenas

LOVE LETTER TO THE OED

Love letter to the OED,
and dictionaries all!
They soothe the soul for wondering minds
when word questions befall!

The Sandman comes—what is that stuff
where sleepy eyes are found?
Well, laugh at this—that sandy stuff,
its real name is GOUND!

For politicians, vile and dumb
another wondrous word:
it's MAWWORM—and a perfect fit
for hypocrites absurd!

And see that cobweb in the hall—
though cob you've never seen?
From 14th century from coppe to cobbe
COB is that spider being.

Plus BULLY-SCRIBBLER—such a noun
from writers small and bitter.
Though much of this we see today—
cycling now on Twitter!

To cover blemish with make-up,
an action verb—oh yes!
To FARD, to over-FARD's not hard!
I've done it I confess.

Combo Greek word with rock plus gods;
and PETRICHOR, the name.
It's Earth's first springtime sweetest smell—
that Heavenly first rain!

So many words, so little time
so people—do not tarry.
To educate, confound or laugh—
LOVE THAT DICTIONARY!!

--Gloriana Casey

ONE SUMMER DAY

Snake:

Wispy snake of silver smoke—a question mark—peers over the
mountain;
then coils, undulates, touching gently the mountain top.
Its smoky tongue, kisses, caresses the earth—the smoke cloud
grows, Tongue becomes arms—become hands—become fingers.

Forms Reassemble:

A swirl of smoke envelops the mountainside!
Rising high, this massive cloud, leans down and bites into the earth.
Its smoky yawn turns into a gaping hole of angry mouth.
Flares fall lightly, delicately, clinging to their single, blade of dry grass.

A Dance in Slow Motion:

A minuet then turn, and limbo down! Rumba! Rumba!
Blades of grass flicker into ancient warriors of Time, singing
crackling shrieks and marching with frenzied feet.
Flaming fingers snap and grasp in a furious Bacchanalia to Oxygen.

Frenzy! Riot! Anarchy of the Grass:

In this Holy Grail of land and forest, trees become torches—Sunset
comes at midnight—the holocaust of the hills rages on!
ARSON! ARSON," scream the singed and homeless jays as
Golden Hills turn to ashes—and ashes turn to dust.

--Gloriana Casey

THE BLUE EMPTINESS

on the last day
of the world
she lay on her bed
slightly elevated in
a convalescent hospital
her children and grandchildren
really really loved her
but there were jobs,
babies and puppies
to consider

next to her was
a woman with Alzheimer's
who smiled vacantly
and never remembered her name
the smell was odious—
urine and disinfectant –

she surrendered to her pillow
and let her eyes close
instantly her brain was invaded
by roses and daisies
their long roots anchored
to her nerve endings

then the sky swept
away all flowers
dazzling her with its
blue blue emptiness
she could see but
was not seen
she saw children
running in the distance
and as the birds
began to sing
she drifted away

on lazy clouds
leaving the old
world of pain
for a new world
both rich and strange

--Peggy Castro

MY BROTHER'S DEATH

He is like a broken clock that is still ticking.

He is a moon that stares faceless
out into the darkness,
and the night after he died, I felt
him whisper in my ear.

He called no one.
He is a magic trick
that is about to disappear
under the card table.

He is a puppet
whose strings are pulled
by the troubled branches
of dead, snarled trees.

I saw handprints
of the blood of wild mustangs
dancing down the hall
where he staggered and leaned
on his death march toward heaven.

--Chuka Susan Chesney

Originally published in *The Fourteenth Annual Poet-Artist Collaboration*.
March 30 - May 9, 2015, Crossings at Carnegie, Zumbrota, MN.

WANTING TO BE WITH YOU

If you are a disease
I shall seek no immunity
but cherish every symptom
every ounce of pain

If you are a defect
I shall be a flawed diamond
eager to shine
despite my black center

If you are a missing piece
I shall be a crescent moon
delighting in my deficiency

If you are distance
I shall be a lost traveler
never arriving my destination

If you are misery
I shall be clinically depressed
moping and crying all day

If you are death
I shall be terminally ill
kissing and embracing the Grim Reaper
counting down the days

--Jackie Chou

LOUISA

Louisa puts her shoes on the wrong feet.
How can she walk with her toes angled sideways?
What will happen to Nana
when she gets it right?
Louisa is my childhood.
She is the warm sun I didn't feel.

"I love everybody."
Minutes after she was born, she turned towards me
in the little room on the fifth floor of Kaiser Sunset
Her eyes clear, peering out from birth.
She's been watching me for 6 and ½ years.

No one ever looked at me before.
She looks at her own face in the mirror.
"I'm adorable."
What will happen to Nana?

Louisa lives inside stories.
In that special place
at the end of her thumb. Eyes glaring, she says, "I need my privacy."
What will happen to Nana?

Between the top of the refrigerator and the ceiling
is where you go when you die.
Last night, she asked her papa to hoist her up there.
"I'm an Angel in Heaven."
The glare of the light caught her hair in a halo.
What will happen to Nana
when that space is a sticky film of dust?

"Tonight both my parents died
and you can't be my grandmother any more,
you have to be my mother.
Sometimes you are very nice
and sometimes you are very strict."

It's been a while since she asked me
to tie long silk scarf on the top of her head
so she could toss her hair from the tower like Rapunzel.
Now she reads on her own.
"Nana, it says, 'No food allowed.'"

She put her shoes on right.
What will happen to Nana?

--Marsha Cifarelli

FOOD FOR THOUGHT

I am craving you
Like summer flowers crave the rain
A feverish famine explodes in my brain
But my stomach doesn't growl, nor is it food that I seek
It's your touch, your kiss, your making me weak
For sensations so intense
A passion so pure
Fueling my hunger, begging for more
Of you and me, a buffet of delight
Savoring each other
Day into night
Night into day, I want to feast at your feet
Hot, cold, bitter, sweet
It doesn't matter the type of sustenance
As long as it relieves my pain
So feed me, feed me again and again
With your love
With your love
With your love

--Jihan Coleman

PRESENT FROM THE PAST

We tramp past Wordsworth's daffs and dales,
the dark cramped table where Jane worked
her bit of ivory, hear the chirk
and quack of Beatrix's tales,
watch black-sheep-dotted, windswept Wales
awaken, scale its rain-slicked cirques,
stride Yorkshire's moors of mist and murk,
bleak tracks becoming humming rails
'neath London's wheeling streets, her hustle,
tongues and Thames, gray raiment, wander
Edinburgh, all burr and bustle,
"Scots wha' hae." And ever under
now there whispers *then*, their rustle,
past in present, never sundered.

--Stephen Colley

REVERSAL

Stolen moments tunneled
into evaporation of a year.

A lifetime of hunger spurred
from the single drop of one
taste.

Caught in a dream
where all doors lead
to a basement.

We won at failing
ourselves in slow motion

Grabbed for a finish line as it
slunk like a sidewinder
across sands.

Observations made us
ignorant. Every mile drew us
deeper into a pit of being lost

Until we returned to the
moment before our first
breath, before the first

burst of cold air taught
us how to cry.

--Beverly M. Collins

BETWEEN RIDDLES

Some stages in life are much like
A riddle-of-a-walk-between-worlds.
A neither-here-nor-there place.
This feeling of frozen waits like a
Sneeze that interrupts, then does
Not come.

A sudden-sharp-pang of hunger
That disappears without a feeding
Or thirst that waters itself into
Quenching.

Some of us approach life as if we
Have 250 years to swim through our
"Got to do" list. While the "Really want
to do" list looks on in pregnant pause.

We are a belly-laugh-with-legs silenced
Before a sober daybreak and the quake of
A peaceful nightfall. Why do so many
Of us make our desires a priority for the
Next lifetime... maybe?

Is acquisition of a dream a dark drowning
Pool for some? Do we fear our truest,
Deepest desires are the bridges that take
Us under?

--Beverly M. Collins

MASHED POTATOES

Crumpled leaf air
Pavement spent of heat
The naked crunch
of ground
No cover
of words,
doors, footsteps
except yours
Breathing
because you're all finished
Work, and stuff, and dinner
Nothing left
and no light to look at it
And as you suck in a
breath
and turn
to go find something,
to start another
small machine,
again,
you find a light
It surprises you,
even though it's supposed
to be there
Even though
you've seen it before
over the crumpling leaves,
the cords
the stuff,
that water-color painted
glow,
round, geometric
and shifting

the moon
And you hold on it
to trap that first awe
but it passes so fast
Sometimes the moon catches you off guard
like when mashed potatoes are delicious
See you later, moon
I'll catch you later

--Marshel Copple

TWO STAIRWAYS

The first greets those who promenade
through the foyer to a sunken

living room; its steps—wide with
carpeted tread—ease beneath gilded panels

lined with portraits of staid patriarchs
long dead. Bright red lips brush fair cheeks,

besitos de cultura alto,
as these elegant guests parade

through the living room past a massive
dining table and walls affixed

with innocuous ceramic buttons,
doorbell fixtures to summon the help

from the kitchen hiding a second staircase:
steep, jagged, and above all concrete.

Servants—rough hands wrapped in skin darker
than the mahogany furniture

they rub to a high shine—trudge between floors
carrying the weight of meals, loads of laundry,

flutes of lemon water, and whispered curses,
triggered by constant buzzing commands.

Meanwhile, quiet worms of hate burrow, deep
yet imperceptible, into their hearts.

--Bill Cushing

POETRY IS... PRAYER

Wild but tempered
Windy foot soldiers'
       Thought-movement
A pen crosses a page
       (Teases, teasing, teased)
Rivers of lines strike white
Ink penetrates
       (One leaf floats)
       At the river's edge, catches light before
       (We hear it)
       Sun spots have sound,
Sparks that travel
From the nitrogen rich pulse,
       (Rhythmic)
Benefits the soggy soul groping
       (Grope, gropes, groped)
Like goggles under glass
Charging through the mud of experience
       Naming, ordering and expanding
It's arrow's tune
       Piercing our collective soul
       (To see again),
And it's simple food.
Churned and chewed,
On that freeway of a life,
       Lives lived and living,
       (Yours, mine, his, hers, theirs)
Noisily informing
       (inform, informs, informed)
The unbroken peptide chain legacy of
       Thoughts' movement
Intruding our Now
With yours, the Poet
       In the space between atoms

--Devo Cutler-Rubenstein

AFGHAN OF STARS

Crouched low to the earth
    but not like a lion
    or beast stalking prey,
like a lost child
    finding herself, alone
    atop a sand dune
    under an afghan of stars.
I no longer wonder why
    I am
    all that I am not
    right now,
but my body craves the question
    like an infant reaches for food,
why must I live
    like a flower dying
    to bloom?

--Stacy DeGroot

CIRCA '69

We blow out of Twentynine Palms by summer
sail toward the smoke signal that rises in the west
moving under low skies which flicker, black out,
explode, and clear just long enough to stow our key.

We boat waves of asphalt, the split strip a river, as
wind smooths our faces, crackles over desert,
kicks up grit and scented straw in the wake of
a speeding semi, its bowels a holocaust of cows.

Wind turns a mill in the valley that wobbles
spins iridescent, pinwheel Play-Doh comic peel.
It lifts mirror images, funhouse distorted,
ourselves in ink, elevated and warped.

Wind sears; driver's eyes droop; he turns, asks:
"What do you want them to say at your funeral?"
"Start the car," I urge. "'Start the car'?" he echoes.
"Crank it and I'll tell you about my funerary theme."

He shifts, lurches forward, unaccustomed to
wrangling this pony altered. The cat in the catapult,
Freedom our hitchhiker, pipes up — spirited
roadside wildflower picked in Joshua Tree.

She'd offered. (We should've asked what it was
before chasing it with the last of our Boone's Farm).
"At my funeral, I want them to say, 'She was kind.
And *beautiful!* She lived fast, died young, left behind

This gorgeous corpse!'" then purrs and dithers.
The driver coaxes the Mustang into a full gallop, yells:
"As for me, I want them to say, 'He was wise!
a true survivor, who left behind this exhausted cadaver

well-worn with the good use of years!'" We dodge a
gauntlet of trucks, fall behind a battalion of reinforced
American models. Eyes leer, quiz us in our convertible.
Its contents, jettisoned by Freedom, trail in our wake.

"What about you," the driver nudges, "*your* funeral?"
I pause. Tail lights swirl, throb bright as the velvet that'll
line my coffin. "I want them to say, I want them to say,
'Look, he's moving!'"

--Seven Dhar

WOMAN IN BLACK

On my eighth birthday
as the neighborhood kids
pin the tail on the donkey
Daddy says
Look who's here!

A woman in black
stands on the corner
a sad statue holding
a long box with red bow
she hands to me.

Inside is the walking doll
I begged Daddy for
What do you say?
he reminds me
I repeat the magic words

*Why don't you
give your mother a hug?*
Although it's warm out
she's wearing a thick coat
I put my arms around her waist

Everything is lumpy and hard
She doesn't hug me back
Daddy asks *Would you like to come in?*
No, she nods, turns
walks slowly back to the car

Though she is silent
through the glass
I see those empty eyes
staring at me
as they drive her away

I never loved
that doll
walked with her a few times
then put her
back in the box

--Pauli Dutton

ALL OUR LIFETIMES

tonight, from my bed,
I hear *please forgive me*
not the message I'd craved
still it comforts
triggers an urgency

yes, I declare
there's no other way
will you forgive me
for the mistakes I made
during all our lifetimes?

of course, the voice sounds surprised
I confess we'll surely need
to do this again
that's okay, the voice answers
we have forever

--Pauli Dutton

THE FOOD OF MY LIFE

No money days of WWII (Mom cooked)
      Enormous appetite
      Peanut butter sandwiches
      Milk and cereal
      Soup Summertime Victory Garden vegetables
      Hot dogs 12 cents Hamburgers 15 cents
      Skinny as a bone
      I knew we would go to war with Russia next

Cold war expense account at North American Aviation
      Standard lunch
      Filet mignon
      Baked potato
      Wine
      Cheesecake
      Gourmet Society for the Leisure Arts
      Forum of the Twelve Caesars
      Mobile Guide top restaurants
      Russian Tea Room
      Up to 192 pounds
      I knew we would not go to war with Russia

Budget Crisis and 9/11
      Fighting cancer
      Greens
      Sprouted grains
      Yogurt
      Salmon
      Sardines
      Cut saturated fats
      Walking lost weight
      Pneumonia helped – to 147 pounds
      If they asked me to fight in Iraq
      They would know I could not run away

--Richard Dutton

DUST

I'm no roster of credentials
Just the bare essentials
In a slowly moving matrix
Where mountains over time
Become an apparent dominatrix

But mountains know much better
Pressuring each prescient stone
Which meta-morphs and meta-dwarfs
Into rust and dust, while all alone

Pushing through to mountains' crown
Pushing mountains upside down
I'm no roster of credentials
Just the bare essentials

--Lynn Fayne

GRETEL

These days, even the screech
Of a fork in the garbage disposal
Reaches to memories
Of a snaggle-nosed woman in preacher black
Hawking candy-colored mushrooms among the beech trees

These days, even the crunch
Of dried mud on the newly-cleaned carpet
Recalls how a trail
Of crumbs and hunches
Could guide you home safe from the teeth-laden shade

These days, even the squeal
Of recalcitrant grocery cart wheels
Sneaks you back to when
Clever words and a strong push
Were all that you needed to steal the gold and win the deal

But these days
Chores crowd you from your path
And the buzz of responsibilities
Drowns out the whispering call
Of sweets waiting to be bitten

--Katherine Footracer

THERE IS A SEASON

Autumn comes
She recedes with the sun
Height first
Then her world as she ventures out only for pet food and day-old
pastries
Her memories dry up and crunch underfoot
Curiosity and vocabulary blow away on Santa Ana winds
Thanksgiving comes
She shrivels
I give thanks for even that small presence
Winter nears
She forgets not just my name, but who I am
Christmas comes
She remembers that I love her
Christmas goes
Her speech ebbs
But does not return like a tide to raze defiant sandcastles
She makes no sense and leaves home in an ambulance
She returns one week later, again in an ambulance
Winter deepens
Her breathing changes so I leave work to sit with her
Her pulse is too fast, then too slow and then slower still
Her hand in mine, I ease her onward
I drink caffeine and alcohol for two weeks
Winter lightens
I water my garden and myself
California poppies that she loved
but could never get to grow in her yard
burst forth in mine
I laugh without shadows
Spring has arrived

--Katherine Footracer

SYNCHRONICITY

I dreamt I was in San Francisco again, looking out the bay window at the apartment across the street where we once lived, where our friends now live.

I thought how nice to be back and to be in Altadena, the best of two possible worlds.

You came in, my husband – which one were you? – Don, maybe John? – and utterly pleasant, without the old tension, said, "I want some Indian pizza" – which was exactly what I wanted. You said you'd go down to the corner and get some, which made me even happier.

The kids were sleeping in the back bedroom, and the ghost cat snuggled next to our new dog.

I thought how perfect everything is. We were young, and no less wise than we are now.

> split open
> pomegranate
> red jewels glisten
> among membranes
> of memory

--Joyce Futa

Originally published in *Lit Windows: A Book of Haibun and Tanka Prose,* by Joyce Futa (Blue Light Press: 2017).

SALT CURE

We walk along the edge of continents
surrounded by water
the taste of salt on our tongues,
blue sound and fury in our head,
and the sun glittering
on vast variations of ocean.

It's all so much to take in,
we squint our eyes
walking for miles on the beach.
Blood runs its rivers through the body,
ions stipple the brain,
making us think
then not think.

On one side is the city.
After the election
people in shock
walk on sidewalks, sit in buses,
pace rooms of skyscrapers.

On the other side
huge and tiny creatures move
through dark mysteries of ocean,
silk bodies sliding
through silk seaweed and water.

As we walk and walk,
everything simplifies
for one short moment
to a pure line of horizon,
the half ocean, half sky.

--Joyce Futa

Published in *Earth Music*, poems from the Blue Light Press Summer Workshop, 2017.

MAN WITH COCKATOO

If I were dreaming I would talk to the man who often walks up my street with a white cockatoo on his leather-bound arm. The man looks ascetic, small and lean, a bit like my father in an alternate universe, without wife or children. I've never tried to speak to him, and he never acknowledges me and my dog. But I understand. How can he think of anything but what he carries, that solid magical idol of snowy purity? And what could I say to such a pair? Do I have questions for which I need answers?

But in the world that is my dream, I say "Blessings, dear shaman, homage to your bird!" and watch him turn onto mythic streets, pixelating into stars.

> stranger
> you say
> there are many ways
> to simply love
> in this multifarious world

--Joyce Futa

Published in *Lit Windows: A Book of Haibun and Tanka Prose,* by Joyce Futa (Blue Light Press: 2017).

WHEN I CRY

I cry when children go hungry each day;
I cry when children are sad for the loss of their parents.
When I cry, I cry because tears are healthier than rage.
I cry when justice isn't the meal of the poor;
I cry when the disenfranchised keep getting slapped.
I cry when crimes against the poor go unpunished.
I cry when only the privileged have a voice.
I cry when I see nothing but chaos around me.
I cry for justice I never got.
I cry when others see me brown but not human;
when you become brown you'll understand my tears.
My heart and I cry for the world in danger.
I cry for those whose voice is still being silenced
because my brain already cried and bled for it.
When I cry, my heart still beats
because it once almost didn't.
I cry when I'm asleep, and I cry when I'm awake,
because once I was neither asleep nor awake.
I cry when I realize inner strength and perseverance
are the victors of relentless struggles.
I cry for the poor who have nothing but give all
and cry for the rich who have much but share nothing.
When I cry, my soul rests, but my heart yearns
for peace and the survival of humankind.
I cry for a world devoid of love.
I cry for answers I see in my mind
and hope someday will come true.

--Martina Robles Gallegos

HOME IN A BUCKET

Once I saw a little creeper napping in a bucket;
scared me half to death and made me make a racket.
I took a second look, and it looked kind of cute.
I'm glad I didn't whack it.
It was a green-yellow caterpillar
snuggled in its blanket, er, cocoon.
I'm going to watch this creature
from midnight until noon.
Now I know why all the leaves have holes.
If this critter won't stop eating,
it'll look like two fat moles!
What if it eats the entire bucket?
I'll put it in a rocket and…Boom!…To the moon!
Don't worry, it won't be cold;
I'll load up its cocoon.
I hope that silly bucket keeps growing caterpillars;
I like the royal kind:
Let them be Monarchs!
I wonder how many butterflies
will make it home in this bucket?
An entire kingdom!

--Martina Robles Gallegos

Originally published in a prior version in *Altadena Poetry* online on June 6, 2017.

HE THINKS OF PINK MOSCATO WITH A LEMON SLICE

The smoke is thick
Barstool uncomfortable
Hours of sitting and thinking
Muffled background music
Drinks ordered
Glasses clicking
Quiet private conversations
Surrounding him sitting alone

"White wine please!"
Someone cheerful orders
Startled, he looks up, glances around
Surveys the room
Lights another cigarette
Sips his cold beer
Moves restlessly on the barstool
Picks up his car keys

She should have been here
Her favorite drink is Pink Moscato
With a lemon slice

--Mary L. Gigger

AFTER

It was hard
To erase you
From the phone book
To scratch you off the
Christmas list

Difficult to avoid
The path worn to your door
Check the flood of memories
The reminder of your eyes
The tilt of your head, your laugh

Your absence haunts the world
Where I live still
But you are gone
What could have been
Nags at my soul

I was unprepared
For what comes after...
After you are no more

--Esther Gillies

ENCAPSULATED

aerobics students
drive around the parking lot
twenty-five minutes
looking for parking spaces
close to the gym entrance....

encapsulated
high atop moon rocket
sweating astronaut
ponders, calls mission control—
why give contract to low bidder?

--Charles Harmon

MEDITATION ON A SUPER MOON

Oh, Super Moon hanging so large
and luminous in the sky
I gaze at you and wonder
are you a lantern made to light the way
for ships lost at sea, or the lens
of a great telescope
from a distant galaxy, or
are you Earth's faithful lover
come to bathe her tonight
in your ineffable light?

--Hazel Clayton Harrison

Originally published in *Journal of Modern Poetry 20*: 2017 (Chicago Poetry Press, April 2017).

SAND DRAWING

I watched a sect of Buddhist monks
draw a mandala made of colored sands.

With skillful hands, they drew gardens, temples
designs so divine, like stars in the heavens
they shined.

When the monks were done, to my dismay
one took a brush and swept it all away.

When I asked him what that meant
he said, *Existence is impermanent.*

Now when I look at my house, my car
my reflection in a looking glass

I remember what that wise man said
Someday they will all pass.

--Hazel Clayton Harrison

SAFETY NET

As a little girl,
I felt safe when I lay on the belly
of our Doberman Pinscher Inky.

I could feel the rise and fall of his breath
as his belly cradled my head.

I was safe, secure, protected,
as if cuddled
by Arc Angel Michael himself.

Though I no longer have the belly of Inky
to sooth my discontentment,

I close my eyes,
take long deep breaths,
envision myself surrounded

by bright white light
and listen

for the heartbeat of the Universe
as it rises and falls
within me.

--Teri Hicks

ARRIVAL

Please, come home.
Walk into the door of the kitchen
where stew and wheaten bread
steam, where a fire warms.
Your father will tune the strings,
unwrap the *bodhran*.*
I will uncover the harp.
The stew will simmer.
With hands wiped on my apron
I will open my arms
to you, my firstborn child
so long traveling. Your sisters
will dance. The old ones will smile
through brown, gapped teeth,
will smile blue into your eyes.
Wrapped around you the old songs,
the scent of turf fire, the smell
of our own wool and you will sing.
While you sleep
I will wrap around you a woven shawl
to shield you. Please come home
to bleating lambs,
to the resting place of love.

--Marlene Hitt

---

*The *bodhrán* is an Irish frame drum.
Originally published in *Clocks and Water Drops* (Moonrise Press, 2015).

WOOD MADE OF TREE

Box tree wood
built a house of God,
was carried through the wilderness;
cedar built the home of David,
juniper became an incense prayer.
Mangers were made of wood,
sturdy, to enfold, to nourish.
Wood. Softwood. Hardwood.
Teak and ebony.
Olives branched over for comfort
that one night.
Palm branches led the way
to a cross made from a tree;
the essence of wood, essence
of the tree, of the great oak,
a monument,
heartwood at its core.

--Marlene Hitt

WHO WAS SHE AT THIS POINT?

Who was she at this point?
                    Was she the fixed point?

        The flag on the pointed pole

            Was she the decision to stand firm?

                She was so sure

                So fixed

 One day the fixed point broke

She lost her point
She forgot her flag
She sat down
She felt uncertain

Who was she
Without her point?

--Joan Krieger Hoffman

Hoffman hosted "A Woman's Point of View" on the Cox cable network.

HER WAY

She came
didn't stay long,
long enough that the walls
speak her name on certain days
She came
wearing black
meek and magnetic
olive-skin
wavy-hair
She wore it up
not to tempt us
She came
a raindrop
a rose
moist, fresh, young
with old wisdom
She came
a wise ballerina
She danced between
one-eyed hyenas
men three times her age
She made paper snowflakes
pink and green tulips
winter spring never the same
She came
this daughter of seasons
offered her eyes
that dim-eyes might see
her music to ears searching for peace
Her poetry and lemon-dried humor
silence her strength
Her world
no one could enter
except those who sang her song
her way

--Randel Horton

A SUMMER IN HASHIGÁURA*

I hurry to the sea shore,
transparent turquoise water,
warmth of the sun on my body.

Life opens up, a vast panorama.
Quaint anemone nodding with the tide,
invite me deeper into their abode;

crustaceans try to hide in the
sandy bottom,
intricate coral structures;

combinations of colored fish
defy the imagination.
Everything in motion.

Underwater castles.
Mystery books beneath my feet.

--Gedda Ilves

---

*One of three summer resorts around the city of Darien on the Liaodong Peninsula,
Northeast China.

VANISHING SHADOWS

I am trying to catch
the receding shadows,
the receding shadows
of the summer's adieu;

the summer's adieu
with the vanishing shadows
the shadows that follow me
as I wish you would.

I remember you in concert
your violin sounds,
the music from your violin
penetrated my heart;

your Blue Grotto eyes,
the elegant mauve dress
your eyes and the dress
as you stood on the stage;

the golden liquid moon
over the lake outside
night shadows it cast
on the lake by its light;

the parting summer
with its vanishing shadows
and your image imprinted
so vivid in my mind.

--Gedda Ilves

THIS TIME

Mom said *I'm 94 years old, tired and ready to leave. I'm not giving permission for chemo or to cut on my body. I am living with cancer. I'll die with cancer.* I tell Mom—*I'll see you tomorrow. I love you.* I have a happy and sinking feeling. The next morning, I got "the phone call." Dale, my favorite cousin said, *Your Mom passed away this morning.*

I arrive in Florida that night. Dale, my Mom's executor, picks me up. A new kind of loneliness. It's been years since I visited the family compound where privacy tripped and secrets tip-toed. My mom and her three sisters (all gone) lived shouting distance from each other, first in St. Thomas Virgin Island, New York and three cities in Florida. They were best friends, combative and envious. They took care of each other when illness and need intruded. No backs turned, even when there were long stretches of "I'm not talking to..." My four uncles learned how to be nimble and pivot when dealing with their sisters who were a step or two ahead.

The next morning, we talk over breakfast while sadness, loss and emptiness ebb and flow. Zeslie, one of my Mom's closest friends and Dale followed my mother's explicit written instructions to make sure there would be no loose ends. We visit the funeral home. The director shows me the casket Mom chose years ago. He asked, *Do you want to change it to another one?* I reply, *Even if the casket were heart shaped I am not going against her wishes.*

Dennis, Dale's younger brother invites us for lunch at his home. He is a retired Marine. Cousin Sofia, my oldest cousin and the only smoker in the family arrives. Her sense of humor and thick skin keeps her puffing. She walks with a cane. She survived her husband and youngest son. We eat Virgin Islands food: stewed chicken, pigeon peas and rice, plantains, johnnycake and salad. Our St. Thomian accents fall into place as we catch up and tell stories while silence and glances touch down gently.

The main topic of conversation is my Mom, the beautiful one, complicated, wise, and no-nonsense and crazy-making even when love rode her shoulders bare back. That evening Dale drives to Mom's apartment complex. He asks, *Are you OK staying here by yourself?* I say, *I have to stay— I'm supposed to be here.* It was my first time in her apartment. I feel strange. I look in her closet. Spot a new black dress. It is not her size. I try it on. It fits perfectly.

--Gerda Govine Ituarte

MEMENTO MORI B.J.T.

I have one picture, saved from a friend's phone;
A bad snap, staring at a whited screen,
Blank space amid things I no longer own,
Your face in profile, pensive, caught between
The images' flicker, your inner stage
In the crowd of that pixilated past.
Your eyes gone empty as an unused page
Left blank, reflecting mirrors at half-mast
As though dreaming of parts and lines to learn,
Of new parades and peoples ripe to pen.
Your rapt mourning another's final burn
On prosceniums here, pondering 'when.'
Which came unexpected and quiet to make
This digitized moment my last and your wake.

--Briony James

SOUTHERN ALARUM

Talbots suits and Tieks
tendonitis respects no red sole
perfectly appointed, anointed
polished, primped and prettified
they do not stand but pose
resort wear caryatids
supporting manufactured lawns
static neighborhoods
streets never see stickball or chalk
hear no laughter that hasn't been
well sugared
in happy hour bliss

vertical lines dipping into lipstick-mummification
they try to drawl but crawl back
the flat A of Paramus gives away the game
these Scarletts muster their magnolia moonshine
poised over iced teas
in retirements of plastic privilege
content to glare at black cashiers
while stocking up on Walmart gin and tonic

their charms exist only on bracelets
golden chains for Kiowa Island cages
snakeskin hides shriveling
in their chosen swamp
pretend aristocrats mud larking
in a seditious sea
empty acquisition amid mortal fear
and long-term care beckons
its skeletal arm flung back
like Ahab's ghostly invite
to remind these southern belles
soon their bells will toll

--Briony James

LATIN MASS

I am grateful for the sounds of
barking dogs outside thin windows
at this Equity waiver sized chapel atop East Los Angeles.

Here, every sound can become thunder.
Roosters, airplanes, Banda music out car windows.
I like any sound other than us.

Our pale boys are so much louder
than the boys from the neighborhood.
Everyone from the neighborhood knows it.
I look at them
trying not to look at us.

Latin, Spanish, English all sounds the same
when you're on high alert.

My husband's chants, keep the beasts at bay
while I pray for only this:
To not be that mother—
The one with those boys.

--Sabrina Kaleta

HANKOOK SPA

Signs in Korean and bad English
warn against putting toilet paper in the toilet.
What is it about L.A. and bad plumbing?
The packed earth won't consume all our bile.
It pushes back.

I'm a white girl who hates
the multiplying of white girls
in the spas at K-Town-
as if it's my sole domain
to fumble through the etiquette,
wading through the peppered looks of
confusion and dismay from those here first.

What otherness remains
when we are all here?

In the hot tubs, I read Bukowski
and think of book nerds apoplectic
at the dampening of words in steam and overflow.
But I don't think Hank would mind.

No children can talk to me here,
or husbands, or mothers.
Nothing can be done for anyone.

The book helps guard against those
who would invade this strange bubble.
Most of the older Korean ladies wouldn't be bothered
or don't have the words to bridge this shared space.
It's those ones that look more like me that I worry about.
They think we're in a club.

I let the heat singe their chatter.
They can't come in.
I imbed my feet in the hot clay balls.
A meditation.
No one can come in.

--Sabrina Kaleta

SHOES

Both boys,
shoes on the wrong feet
on purpose.

Yes, this is a test.
Attention, attention.

At Brandeis, grinning fiercely against the cold,
smoking an old man's pipe with cheap tobacco,
I trudged through Massachusetts snow
in patent leather thigh-high boots,
spiderweb tights and a black lace bustier I brought from L.A.–
a walking affront.

Now, when my Target t-shirt is inside out
from 6 am yoga to dinner,
misshapen, slightly torn by indelicate small hands,
it's not so calculated.

I look across the room at four tiny curved-out feet.
Notice me,
and recognize the challenge,
the inbred opposition,
the joke few will get.

--Sabrina Kaleta

ALTADENA, 2014

We search for the lease to our house.

> Breaks in the wind
> rustle of palm fronds

Hands rifle through drawers we will never own.

> Criminal Minds filming
> on our block next week

Simulation of a house fire.

> Emergency vehicles with fake insignia
> intermittent sirens

Tonight, it will be quiet.

> Refrigerator rattle
> consumes the night

You raise our lease like a victory flag.

> The sour cream
> will spoil by morning

It states one pet per household.

> Our two cats look
> so much alike

The landlord will never know them apart.

--Bonnie S. Kaplan

SKID ROW, 4 P.M.

There is screaming in the streets
below, sirens emanate
up seven floors to where I teach.
Every afternoon a crackling

tune draws closer, a relentless
loop of Pop Goes the Weasel.
The Ice Cream Man comes to Sixth
and San Pedro.

They still manufacture Bomb
Pops in striated flavors—cherry, lemon-
lime, and blueberry—summery,
sweet, dripping patriotism

all over the veteran's hand,
the one that still works.
Sometimes the Ice Cream Man
brings his son on the route.

The boy helps deliver Good
Humor Bars to those in wheelchairs
and makes change. Grown-ups assemble
around the truck's window

for frozen Big Sticks,
Fifty-Fifty Bars, King Cones.
There is laughter and blue tongues
and a woman who thinks the Ice

Cream Man is stealing her thoughts—
the layers of peeling stickers
on his truck are evidence enough,
and how he keeps everyone coming back.

--Bonnie S. Kaplan

FACING UP

I came into this world
    kicking my feet and crying lustily (although
    only for a moment or two, they tell me),
    face up
    watery eyes taking in my new surroundings—
      blinking Christmas tree, bustling midwife,
      wide-eyed father—

lying flat on my back.

On my honeymoon,
I entered the virgin unknown territory
    of mystical sensuality (previously forbidden
    yet now expected to embrace and enjoy!)
      with muffled cries of pleasury pain while once again
        I found myself in the familiar position—

lying flat on my back.

Three daughters channeled forth from my insides
    as I clenched my teeth, cried, even—I confess—screamed
      choosing natural childbirth, (a mistake I now admit,
      after watching easy births of grandchildren
      through the medical magic called "epidural"),
    in a position I may have mentioned previously—

lying flat on my back.

And in a coming—yet hopefully far away—day,
    with memories bound up in a white satin pillow
    tied with a bow and placed under my dead head,
  I'll be laid in a decked-out casket
    in a position once again as I began it all,
  (will I watch the descending lid without a cry?)—

lying flat on my back.

--Lorelei Kay

THE PULSING SURF

The surf pounds her white-edged fists
into the sandy beach where I stand.
The sound of slapping water echoes in my ears
as chilled sea breezes whip overhead.

Seagulls shriek and circle above me,
flapping through their frantic air dance
as particles of sand attach themselves
to the soles of my feet.

God stands revealed in the sea —
her white-crested tresses wash the shore clean,
then retreats afar, bouncing kayaks and ships
along the arch of her extended back.

Shimmering in the sun, she laps around islands
and gathers continents in her graceful arms.
Fiercely she holds all life in her pulsing grasp.

Heavy with labor pains, contracting and releasing,
she howls as she births humanity in her depths,
then hurls us onto sandy beaches to crawl
ashore clothed only in her image.

My inborn legacy comes from the depths
of the eternal sea. My every strength and
weakness, rise and fall, I inherit from her.

When my moon wanes, the water will call.
A wave will build momentum, change into a
curling wall of wetness, and roar toward me.

I'll release myself into its white froth
as the ocean eternally pulses, its churning
ebb and flow, its roiling rise and fall —
I'll be transformed, and free.

--Lorelei Kay

WISHING ON A BRAID

Mother-daughter morning ritual,
giggles and wiggles, as I comb
through her long dark hair,

dividing locks into three strands,
while gripping and tugging
at her bobbing head.

First strand over—
How I love
this little girl!

Second strand over—
I hope she'll grow tall,
happy and strong.

Third strand over—
Yet how I wish she'd always
stay small!

Braiding strands together
Love—hope—wish. Love—hope—
wish. Love—hope—wish.

Nearing the end of the braid,
I pull all three lines taut
like my heart strings

and push down on her head.
"Please don't grow up," I whisper
as I fasten the bow.

But she did.

--Lorelei Kay

BABY TALK

for Josie, age two, after reading Madeline for the fifth time in one morning

The sky is streaked with afterthought
the suns's a rheumy eye
you *will* start rhyming, like as not
no matter how you try

Trimeter tries to trip your heels
like toys upon a stair
now baby's found the Easter Seals,
stuck lilies everywhere.

Sated, Datura lilies droop
across the tablecloth
you can't resist that phallic trope –
it rhymes with Phillip Roth

like Portnoy with tinker toy
and Anais with bliss…
for each heroic girl or boy
the quest begins like this.

Oh! how the brain will play its tricks!
Thank the Lord you are there.
Remember this when you are six
and I am who knows where.

--lalo kikiriki

CROSSTOWN: A BUS RIDER'S POEM

When you are old and grey,
sleep will elude you
(even on the slow number 4
to the Westside).
Your thoughts will race
the way your thighs
no longer can and
everything will remind you
        of something else.

Like Ferlinghetti riding on the el,
thinking of Yeats,
Yeats will remind you of Auden,
staring into water,
missing something,
        someone…
                whose name you struggle to recall.

You may not understand,
even if you are "mindful":
on that bus
you cannot tap the thoughts
of your criminal seatmate,
eying an unzipped pocket
        a wallet's bulge.

A girl across the aisle
in a Guns n Roses t-shirt
watches a fly
pummel the big bus window,
        closes her eyes to listen,
                thinks of Death

--lalo kikiriki

ECLIPSE

She lay there
uneasy, shifting
I'm stroking her arm
holding her hand like I did
that day when dad died
she recoils, shifts away
a parade of reluctance
the swollen silly putty
of her skin responds
in a reticent manner
moving
when you aren't watching

her tender arms
tugging at the oxygen tubes
peeling her sheet on
then off
then on
and
off

her upper lip
folded over her top gums
occasionally letting out a raspy, bleating sound
the stench of hunger on her breath
seeps into my nostrils, takes residence there
she is leaving this world as she entered it
with the hunger of a newborn

she had something in her eyes that last day
her retinas a flat, matt, brown
eclipsing her sun
I, on the other side of the moon
no comfort I can offer

no word I can utter
   watching

      my mother

         slip   away.

--Cybele Garcia Kohel

AND NOW I AM HERS

my mom is a girl   a girl again in her senior apartment

where she brings home
shopping carts   parking them in the hallway

full of snack food   for other people

she has pills,   pills she can't remember to take
a girl who doesn't remember
to buy food   for herself
she remembers how to cook   empanadas and instant coffee
she asks cashiers   to write her checks
she spends five dollars   to send her nephew twenty
he has grandkids

Isabel   her name is Isabel
like her mother   the mother she never really knew
the mother who left   her telling her she was worthless
this she never forgets

she always remembers   to hide the wine
because she forgot
she can't have the wine   when she bought the wine
but she remembers to hide it

and I find it in the closet
looking for   her bags to take her shopping.

she does remember me
she's a girl who remembers
she forgot
what she can't remember
the once worthless little girl

her   name   is   Isabel

and she is my mother.

--Cybele Garcia Kohel

POETS LIVE AMONG US

see them
curled up
in a sunny spot
like so many cats
daydreaming
calling
the in-sanctimonious saints
to me! to me!
laying down line and letter
filtering the dull and dormant
through gossamer screens
extracting luminescence, radiance
from sand pebbles
and cadavers of dust
foraging, excavating
as they sit on the metro
as they park in their cars
as they shop for apples
buying time, buying moments
buying back our souls
space by space
letter by letter

--Cybele Garcia Kohel

PANTSUIT IN MY CLOSET

The sun rises, brighter than usual. I put on a robin's egg blue pantsuit to vote with my daughter. I wish my mother were alive.

> suffragette photos
> my grandmother's tiny stitches
> on the quilt block

Darker after the sun sets, the results trickle in. My son calls and whispers, "I don't think she'll win." I count electoral votes in states not yet reporting and tell myself it will be okay.

> election returns
> at a friend's house
> cans of orange crush

I never post a mother-daughter voting photo to FaceBook. I wake up the next morning and wonder where I am. As the months pass, I hear male voices in the crowd as if for the first time.

hervoiceisannoying   notenoughcharismatobepresident
whydidn'tshewearbluejeans   whyBillstrayed

> math degree
> all those men
> I worked with

--Deborah P Kolodji

Originally published in *Contemporary Haibun Today*, Vol 13, No 2, July 2017.

INDIANA NONET*

Sunlight lingers in the fallow fields
perfect rows of cornstalk stubble
shimmer like fine necklace strands
winter tree silhouettes
pen and ink black on
robin egg blue
before spring's
verdant
waves.

--Linda Kraai

---

*A nonet is a nine-line poem, with the first line containing nine syllables, the next
eight, so on until the last line has one syllable.

AFTERMATH

All my life I have been unable to watch violence on the TV or in the movies,
but I watch Ken Burns' and Lynn Novick's documentary "The Vietnam War."

I watch it for my neighbor who returned
from Vietnam a quadriplegic whose family
had to reteach him everything when he came
home . . . his name, the names
of his brothers, how to eat and take
steps with heavy braces along parallel bars.

I watch for my colleague at work
who shook in terror when her husband
just out of medical school
was sent to Vietnam.

I watch it for my friend, widowed young,
whose three sons fled to avoid the war.
when the FBI knocked on her door,
she did not know their whereabouts.

I watch it for the mother
who had lost her only son in Vietnam
who sat next to me on the airplane
when I was flying home for Christmas.
we wept together.

I watch it for those who went
whose coming home was celebrated
by those who loved them best.

I watch it for my cousin
who rode his motorcycle
around the country for two years
after he returned from that war.
He now leads a secluded life.

I watch it for all those etched
in the Vietnam War Memorial . . .
and for generations who will place
flowers and notes beneath their names.

--Linda Kraai

5778: APOLOGY TO A GIRL BOSS*

I'm sorry for talking over you
Or muffling your confident voice
I convinced myself that your ideas weren't worth hearing

I'm sorry for the days I doubted your abilities
For the places I believed you didn't belong
For the times I denied you praise or promotion
And for stopping salary negotiations in their tracks
I believed you couldn't handle a responsibility you had earned

I'm sorry I stopped you from asking questions
I thought you should've already known all the answers

I'm sorry I ignored misogyny in social settings
I encouraged you to degrade other women for your benefit
I'm sorry I told you to step out of the way when a man was in your path
I didn't think you could hold yourself up

I'm sorry for letting men speak over you
For not pushing back when it was assumed
that you would take notes in a meeting
For extracting unnecessary apologies from your lips
And for my silence when old men called you
"honey" "sweetie" and "kid"
I let you believe that silence was better

I'm sorry for placing too big of an importance on your looks
And for valuing the size of your stomach and the width of your hips
Over the size of your brain and the span of your generosity
Even when your heart was full and your actions graceful
I was disappointed when your image wasn't what I believed it should be

I'm sorry for believing that your vulnerability was my weakness
And for viewing your needs through a lens both uncharitable and inflexible
I'm sorry for fearing that your emotions and kindness were liabilities
I'm sorry for searching out flaws and ignoring your strength
I believed every insult while doubting every compliment

I'm sorry I recognized your success as a fluke
And your failure as proof of ineptitude
I'm sorry for every time I denied you credit for a win
And especially for forcing it upon you for a loss

I assumed the worst of you
I expected the best of you
And I demonized you when your best wasn't good enough

I'm sorry for every time I looked at you in the mirror and thought "Impostor"

--Aviva Kraus

---

* The number 5778 is the current Jewish Year, and is a reference to the tradition of making amends and apologizing for one's transgressions during the new year (on Yom Kippur).

SWIPING RIGHT: A SEXTINA

One year I thought about being blonde - would I notice
Whether lighter hair made me stand out in a crowd?
Maybe life can be pursued from a better angle.
But with the summer the lazy heat builds
And the bleach had such an acrid smell
Squirting lemons would have to be enough

Sometimes I try to try hard enough
Ask myself: do you want to be noticed; do you want to notice?
Don't you miss how *good* some boys smell?
So I hope for the best and I jump in: join the crowd.
It'll happen, I tell myself; and the pressure builds
Suddenly I'm judging caption and outfit and filter and angle

I almost said yes until he spelled it "guardian angle"
Nothing he typed after that would've been enough
But I'm only a snob until sexual frustration builds.
Even if I liked one, I doubt I would notice
So I culled from the contingent crowd
Don't pigs find truffles in forests alone by smell?

You know when you're pretty sure you smell
And you're looking for the sneakiest angle
To turn your head and sniff, even in a crowd?
I'd have showered if this morning were long enough
I'd have showered if "drinks?" were given proper notice
The hour approaches and sweat betrays, trepidation builds

All these men with all these faces and all these builds
Swipe for New Car Smell
I remember when all I wanted was a Jake Ryan to notice
Lean against his cherry Porsche - stare at me - eyes piercing –
head at an angle
Am I asking for too much or not enough?
My Fantasy, my Standards, my Reality, and three's a crowd

We grow up believing we're so much more than a face in the crowd
Time, shame, anxiety builds
Having a dog right now is enough!
Okay it's my parents' dog and yes, that's bullshit you smell
But life is about finding a new angle
Right? It's deciding what to ignore and what to notice

The year I turned fourteen I decided it was time for a Signature Smell
My sister said I smelled like baby whore –
not an *entirely* unappealing angle
Right? Anything to make the boys take notice

--Aviva Kraus

PREOCCUPIED

I enter Ross Dress for Less
in search of a vase for birthday roses.
I don't hear the crash
of a 400-square-mile Alaskan glacier
slipping into the sea.

Distracted by thoughts of friends,
to-do lists and journeys to far-away places,
my fingers trace yellow curlicues
on an azure-blue vase.
I can't see the remains
of a 30-acre blue-green
sheet of ice melting in Glacier Park
where I hiked as a child.

At Coffee Bean and Tea Leaf,
absorbed in iced latte and Instagram,
I don't feel the runoff of the
glacier in Antarctica, flowing into the sea.
270 miles of ice, formed over eons,
wiped out in decades.

I stroll down Lake Avenue
and gaze through windows
at gin and tonic happy hours.
I may no longer be here when ocean brine
seeps into cities and islands all over the world
and sinks them off the map.

I'm not thinking about glaciers
retreating like ice cubes in a glass of water
on a record-breaking, global-warming day.
At this moment I'm unaware,
or else I would weep.

--Kitty Kroger

WHAT IS A POEM?

Sometimes I think it's obscurity:
heart slams smoldering forest.
Or is it nature:
daffodils and *waterfalls,*
luminosity pulsating through shimmering leaves?
Sometimes it's rhyme but not always
and when it rhymes, are clichés
OK? Or is this better:
linoleum and *petroleum,*
robotic and *erotic*?
Or near-rhymes like
petrified and low tide?
Are those more dignified?

Is it imagery: *Prussian-blue ball gown,*
salsa on a rooftop in the rain?
Is a poem alliteration like
apple and *angle, simple* and *satisfied*?
Is it fresh words
like *ballyhoo* and *pas de deux*?
Or startling phrases like *searing sting*
and *curious caviar?*
Is it rhythm and beat
like rap and pentameter
Is it a text, a tweet, or a note,
a blog post, a shopping list,
even a birthday card ditty?

Can it be self-expression,
with no rhyme and pulsation,
no imagery and alliteration?
Maybe it's just a first draft,
investigation of destination.

--Kitty Kroger

I SWIM AT NIGHT WITHOUT A BEACON

I swim at night without a beacon
And hear the deadly surf upon the shore.
While most have one, of you, I had none.

I pray hard for the rising of the sun
To warm this dread that chills me to the core.
I swim at night without a beacon.

The clouds obscure the moon upon its run.
The winds rage with the waves' unending roar.
While most have one, of you, I had none.

I long for that sweet time when night is done
And I may something more than loss explore.
I swim at night without a beacon.

I wonder if the past can be undone,
Become a ghost that I do not deplore?
While most have one, of you, I had none.

How is it that you never knew your son
O Father dead and gone as ancient lore?
I swim at night without a beacon.
While most have one, of you, I had none.

--Marc Ladewig

THE KEY

Back home from war,
scarred to the core,
up to a door
a soldier came.

Worn thin with care,
his clothes threadbare,
he listened there
and called her name.

The song inside
went still and died.
With wounded pride
he tried his key.

He came to learn
by twist and turn
the tumblers spurn
to open free.

He thought once more,
kick down the door,
his love implore
on bended knee.

Her love was dead.
He chose instead
to turn his head
and leave the key.

--Marc Ladewig

ON THE CLOSE OF ESCROW

You were their dream house, I guess.
They were pretty sick of the old one,
a lucky buy in the desperate post-war Hollywood real estate market,
close enough to the studio job,
good school, room for a pool,
nice fenced yard for two kids and a dog.
But, with kids gone, a tacky place,
bathroom too cramped for a stand-up pee,
magnolia debris in the pool,
grim uncultured neighbors:
a skin to cast off.
You were shiny and modern—
high on a ridge, Mulholland Drive below—
practically next door to Rudy Vallee's estate.

You weren't *my* house.
My house was that clapboard box on the side of a hill:
half a downstairs for me,
a redwood tree to climb,
a poison-oak-covered slope to shoot arrows into,
bird feeder on the balcony,
a big lawn for earning my allowance.
A true starter house.

Your picture window kills finches
attacking their own reflections;
your cavernous bathrooms echo hums and farts;
no need to climb a tree for a view;
no lawn at all.
No room for me except as a guest.
An ender house.

Last year I became your guardian, your trustee,
payer of your bills, your agent,
your disemboweler.
And, finally,

the encloser of a single key
in a welcome note
mailed to strangers
at your address.

--Peter Larsen

ROTTING MANGOES

Rotting mangoes
aromatic sourness
with rich overtones that change with time
as the ripe, stringy fruit
(no good even for chutney, my mother said,
too turpentiny even to bother tasting)
splat and sprawl and ferment.
Finally: brown smears in the red mud,
squishy stinky salve for bare feet
rough from walking home from school
on hot asphalt.

Eighteen years on, in a foreign village,
I smelled that same smell
and vomeronasal memory took over
as my sinuses filled with it.
My buddies nudged me
ready to move out into the rice paddies.
For a moment I curled my toes in my boots:
phantom squishy texture,
feeling closer to home.

--Peter Larsen

HAIRCUT

A number one on the sides
And a little off the top
The buzzing a swarm of angry bees
Mows neatly past my ears
I wait for the prick of metal on skin
The involuntary jab and jerk of PTSD childhood cuts
Inflicted by my father
Sometimes sober
Sometimes not
The cuts always the same, regardless
My childhood injected with buzz cut pictures
My cranium a pre-teen coconut
Not from choice
But through trial and mostly error
There was a Mohawk once, I believe
The half-remembered vision swimming up
Through thick, repressed memory
My father thought he was saving money
And us
From Ray the Shitty Barber
I am pretty sure that wasn't his real name
But, my father had uttered the name so often
It had become a term of endearment
The tattoo-armed girl swipes the clippers
Quick and sharp
The ink taking on motion in peripheral
A Millennial nickelodeon
I look in the mirror and smile
And wonder what Ray the Shitty Barber's last name was
But think some things are too perfect
To be ruined by answers
My reflection looks more like my father
Day by day
As my thinning, white hair falls in clumps at my feet
Sadness suddenly stares back at me
As I almost wish for one little nick

One small drop of blood
A scarred reminder on my flesh
To take me back again
To be with him one more time
A little more off the top, I say
And the back squared, please

--Rick Leddy

ALWAYS HAVE A PROP, HE INSTRUCTED,
WHEN YOU TELL A STORY OR GIVE A SPEECH

For Tom Thielo

The first ball he held was a baseball
in play with neighborhood kids from the same Brooklyn stoop,
who grew up to become engineers, and move to far places
like California, with a vow never to forget the cloth
from which they came. A day after the stroke he holds
a ball firm in his right hand, the only functional one,
insistent in his grip. The ball given by his granddaughter,
studying to be a teacher of autistic kids. The arc

of his slim elegant fingers, and thumb strength that
of a poised rock climber who scales a wall with reach
and grasp and knows between crevices lay life or death.
His half-moon nails smooth and white against the sheet,
trimmed just a day before by his wife, who waits and prays
steady by his side. Contained within that sphere, all the light
and dark of a lifetime marriage, coiled bands of a well
traveled journey, births of children and grandchildren,
and in this end of awakened mortal life, his last and final prop.

--Kathy Leonard

PRELIMINARY CATASTROPHE BY HOTEL POOL

Grainy image on sixteen-millimeter film
my mother on vacation by the hotel pool
a time when my sister and I still
an unwanted speck in her pretty blue-green eyes
she boasts sporty-slim in a size ten black one-piece
before the corruption of pregnancy to her female form

My father's hand steady as he holds the camera
carefully documents her ritual of preparation
she is deliberate as she tucks dark, seal-like hair
under plastic ruffles of the bathing cap,
stands with pin-up girl posture and sets
pink pedicured toes over the edge of the precipice

She smiles seductive towards the camera,
knows desire moves the man who watches behind the lens
when she leaps, her thin waist taut
all body parts in perfect extension as she breaks the water's surface
as if she were an athlete in a swim lane competition
a race my sister and I will someday lose
only our father the clear winner

--Kathy Leonard

FORESHADOW

Orange and black swirls
of the creator's perfected symmetry
lie on the floor of my garage

I cradle in my hand
the single half of a Monarch-wing
a whole broken into pieces

how dare death
with its sudden gust of wind
come so easily

with one thrust of a bird's beak
still this once bright being into an endless sky
how we are one in this fragility

in this moment, I wear it like a crown
what is left behind comes for all
sudden and undeserved

--Kathy Leonard

MIRROR

One night I stood naked
in front of my mirror

running my hands
over my body,

my thoughts over
in my mind.

My eyes met.
For the first time

I met
the woman I really am.

Face to face
I awaited the moment of vulnerability.

As the tear rolled down
I watched it fall on my breast.

I felt the wetness,
and the weakness.

The ache of emptiness.
I closed my eyes for a moment

and remembered the feeling
of melting into a lover's hug.

When I opened my eyes there was a child before me.
She cannot understand the need.

--Lisa Lewis

HUTS

Whenever we bumped along in Dad's antique Ford
Towards a new town, for a few months, maybe a year,
We – Philip and me – always built a hut.
In the woods, where cranks couldn't spy on us.
The planks we needed for our walls we stole
From rotting woodpiles and long-deserted houses.
When we stayed in Florida – for us, Paradise –
We wove our roof from fallen palm branches
And sharp palmettos. Nice and shady.
Never a door, just a square space to crawl in,
Room to stand. Each hut, we agreed, looked
More complete than those stupid cathedrals in the city.
We sometimes slept there with our stray mutt Lucky,
Classified by a funny vet as a "Heinz 57,"
Which made us laugh. We climbed trees barefoot
For lunch, mangoesguavasbananasoranges.
For dinner we had to go home (napkins, stew).
When we found a school in a town, we went.
It felt odd, all those kids with shoes,
With no secrets.

--Nancy Lind

NO TIME FOR AUTUMN LONELINESS

f
  a   l
    l l ing   e
                    aves
no time
for autumn loneliness

 through the long night
the autumn wind taps out
  its own Morse code

maple leaves
 rush toward winter
  autumn wind

--E. Luke

In Yuki Teikei, Geppo, SoCalHaiku Study Group Anthologies.

A HAPPIER ENDING FOR MOM

I tried to get my family to boycott the movie *Titanic* to avoid the prolonged dying scenes. Because they disagreed, when the ship hit the ice berg, I left to see a remake of the old-time comedy *Small Town Crooks*. When I returned, people were still drowning, and the audience was sniffling and crying, even the men. This incident took place on Christmas Eve in 1998 when my youngest daughter was eight. At midnight she sleepwalked to a neighbor's house, knocked on their door, and asked for her Christmas pony. They were still up wrapping presents, called, and gave us our happy ending.

mom boycotts
Titanic film
no happy ending
for mothers and babes
frozen in the sea

--Janis Albright Lukstein

WHEN GOD LIVED IN BROOKLYN

There was a time when God lived in Brooklyn.
He had bodega on Schermerhorn street
next to a tire repair shop.
I saw Him once waiting for the D train
there was a copper stain
creeping up His garment,
no one seemed to notice but me.
He was a rock star in the seventies,
everyone wanted to be seen with Him,
He couldn't leave his house.
He had to hide
like some mafia don
under a pair of sun glasses.
They made movies about Him then,
people had to wait in long lines to get in.
Then the nineties came and that's that.
He lives in Florida now
traded in His snow shovel
for a pair of binoculars.
His number is unlisted.

--Joe Lusnia

NOT WRITING ENOUGH POETRY

My head is buried
In the mundane
Musings of existence

Balls that rise too fast
And drop quickly

Beauty is lost
Original voices silenced

Sloth as much a part
Of the day as purpose

Where are the poets?
The meddling muses?
The warring words?

Caught in a whirlwind
Of washing machines
And house liens

Neither
Inspiring ink

Slowly I climb back
Into the chair

Where filling the blank page
Is nothing more than
An urge

--Radomir Vojtech Luza

HANDS

I massage organic Trader Joe's coconut oil
on my father's right ankle.
In their bedroom, his leg extends as groans escape his body.
It is past our dinner time—he is waiting for my mother's return
and I have been home all week, witnessing the sympathy of his aches,
how each exposed knuckle hurts.
His knees can't handle his work.
But he works,
because he does not accrue sick time.
Each year, he pays a fine to not have health insurance
because health insurance is too expensive and he has a house to keep.
So he lays in his CA king bed
as his daughter rubs the ankle.
He fell from a roof once, almost killed himself, working.
Sometimes I wonder if he would rather be dead,
then I remember how he enjoys dates and lavash and a gulp of tea.
Suddenly he is most content.
I rub his ankle and even then he worries for my hands.
Tells me to stop.
This is when I know how much this man loves me--
enough to keep his aches from ever touching his daughter's
Hands.

--Karineh Mahdessian

MEA CULPA

Sorry rolls off her tongue easily
As though it was her anointed name
She was born girl in a world where
Girl was shame and soft and weak and hurt

Sorry rolls off her tongue
As though her mouth was made to hold it
Allow her to taste it despite herself
Because she was born

Sorry rolls off her tongue
It's how she loves
Always with apology

Sorry rolls off her tongue
Drapes her skin
So she wears it as her little black dress
Ready to dance
Ready to dine
Ready
Always
Ready and quick to show off
That she understands

Sorry rolls off her tongue
Sometimes, desperate, she wants
To cut off her tongue
So sorry no longer
Has a home

--Karineh Mahdessian

MIND A PLACE OF DANGER

A self-generated prison cell
an invisible bubble of protection
with lies
I am too busy
no time
separating us efficiently
from others
issuing a license
to stay untouched
insensitive
self-important
but alone
our own kingdom
no room
for anyone else.

The mind is a machine
of mass destruction

Earphones
make us deaf
to cries for help
technology toys
replace friends and family
addictions
become our only passion
craving more and more
enjoying less and less
empty and numb
chasing through
the labyrinths
of alienation
with no name

--Mira N. Matarić

SHORT SONGS

smoke grey wisps
wrap morning peaks
sun sleeps
past noon
Pasadena spring
***

irises on the brink
of bloom hesitate
spring is full of caprice
***

red silk pouches swing
below ivory *netsukes*
art of the small on view
on men of Edo
in kimonos without pockets
***

wired by fate
busy ant
scours the kitchen
waggles the news –
crumbs abound
***

--Pat Murphy McClelland

TURNABOUT

The moon, all yin
skillful in the art
of phased presenting,
slow in her risings,
measured in increase,
dark, subtle, temperamental
lately showed
a different face
in her near-total
eclipse of all-yang sun.

Playing out her
passing role
on the diurnal stage,
she altered day's
light hours before –
turned it silver
tinged with green
ominous, dense, serene
and cloaked the solar
body sphere in black.

Stirred by the rare
supernal glow,
she took the lead
and made him feel
slow, deep, tidal, phased
lunar like a woman.

--Pat Murphy McClelland

AFTER CHARLOTTESVILLE

Jewish star locket
Hidden away
American boomer
Found it today
Fondles it gently
And sheds a tear
Then tucks it back
With dread and fear
The lesson's learned
And history will know
Like Grandma before her
She can't let it show.

--Alice Meerson

TENDER

lonely weathered face
kindly soul with tender hands
cradles tiny pup

--Jill Meunier

COWBOY

gruff cowboy visage
tiny dog
in his pocket

--Jill Meunier

A WISH UPON A DOG

I want a dog
To make my world complete
My landlord says no
But that's not a cause for defeat
I'll just keep trying to push the notion
Way before my heart is broken
'Cuz I just cannot afford to move
I'm here for a while and in the groove
Sometimes I feel so very alone
Looking to find that cuddly BONE
A kindly friend will get me through the fog
'Cuz I just wanna get a dog

--Jill Meunier

PORTRAIT OF MY FATHER, 22, WIFE BESIDE HIM

In the background, just behind him
and his new wife, stands the place
where they made love or sex for
the first time, grappling each other
nervously, as if fighting some fresh
beast they'd never seen or heard about.
The Plaza Hotel: where she took a long
hot bath and scrubbed herself red
because her mother said men like a
woman who smells clean, where she
dried and brushed her dark brown
hair until it fell just right below her
back all neatly for him, for he who
would take what she'd been guarding
ever since she knew she had it.

It is morning and both of them are smiling,
looking at the camera as though it
were a funny aunt or a giggling baby.
With his mustache and his hair combed
back, my father stands in his new shoes,
light pants and creased up shirt knowing
that he'd want to put this picture in a
giant frame or at least beside his bed to
see each dawn, work on the horizon.

He is twenty-two, likes the way his wife's
name, Elizabeth, rolls off the tongue
and onto his lips. Likes that she is already
trying to speak English and the way her
words come out half pretty and half ugly
like moths rushing out of her throat. I want
to leave them there like that, as steady
as they look inside that faded picture. I
want to see what lives can have before

the roots get dry or quitted from them.
There, behind frame and glass, they are
happy and in a few months they'll be
down in Baja on some beach, me in
her belly and he singing to her about
food or family or love – that thing that
passes by in such a hurry, like an
inattentive tourist looking for a better
place to see, as if there were such a
place to go.

--Kyle Moreno

CROSSING AGAIN, AND AGAIN

Cathedrals in Mexico used to remind
me of my grandmother – jagged cracks
on the outside and silence on the inside –

until she pulled me to her one warm
day along the foamy coast of Rosarito
Beach and told me she had slept with

my grandfather because of his 1967
Chevy Nova and his thick thick
mustache that curved toward his chin.

I was eleven then. Didn't understand the
philosophy behind having one too many
beers. Couldn't understand why she

was glassy-eyed and redder than usual.
All I knew was this new word she had
put into my mouth like a piece of smooth

chocolate: *Sexo. Sexo.* I asked my mother
what it meant but, widening her eyes and
pulling the drinks from grandmother, she

dismissed it. Besides the way the seagulls
cried and the fat pink shrimp I had for lunch
that day, I remember that my grandmother

said something about how everyone has an
animal inside them. That her husband was,
had been, a tiger. That he had made her a

woman. I know what this means now, and
because I know it has become a memory I
like to taste, in the back of my mind, just as

I would taste a bowl of beefy stew or the
ear of a gorgeous woman and it's why
I keep on crossing, again and again,
into the land of my grandmother.
Into the land of my grandfather.

Into myself.

--Kyle Moreno

THE LITTLE WOODEN BUNGALOW CAME DOWN

overnight – reduced to a stack of cabinets,
stained glass, the elegant wreckage of crown
molding and mahogany banisters.

The swarming scaffold is my new neighbor,
and a century old American dream
is in the pile driver. As the day laborers
quickly haul away the last splintered beam,

the scaffold crew constructs a monolith.

--Kyle Moreno

SUMMERS OF COLLEGE

In summers of college I carried
trays of food or two coffee cups
in one hand or four platters
up my arm. A short polyester tan
colored uniform melted
to my newly bloomed body as I pinballed
around the packed Pennsylvania diner
from table to minestrone soup
to rice pudding, and finally
to the narrow opening of counter
where the club sandwich platters
appeared with young Greek
cooks holding on to one end only
releasing when I made eye
contact, wolves hungry for American
girls. Those days I blushed easily
but no one noticed, the kitchen
was always steaming, the heat
made us all a little uncivilized.

Sitting at the counter Eddie watched
me as I poured his coffee, called me
college girl, tried to tease a smile.
His truck driver compact body, black
curly hair and warm browns
for eyes, a slight chip on a front
tooth. He knew it
was a summer thing, picking me
up in his car the size of Montana
taking me nowhere and everywhere.
The slide into heat and sweetness like
the slowest quicksand. He knew
there is a time and there is a place
for some things and they don't
go beyond that, as if surrounded
by barbed wire, electrified. He knew

he would not be visiting me
in the fall at the liberal
arts college in upstate NY.
I sensed he was right but argued
anyway, like a child that just has
to ask. But anything
less seemed cruel.

--Nancy Murphy

KERN RIVER
I'll never swim Kern River again
     --Merle Haggard

The fish that caught my hook that day
was lured by Velveeta
a soft lump of gold
on an arc of silver
dangling in the river
that Merle sang about.
Only this was a kinder day
with slower, gentler rush
and the quick snag,
my rod bent, tugged down
with a thump of new weight
and almost jerked away
until I backed, pulled the straining rod up
and reeled out
that wiggling slash
glowing like wet neon
that my dad netted
swirled in the stream
and laid on ice.
And Dad in his baseball hat
and my brothers in their cowboys
were all veteran fishers
But this was a soft day
when the sun washed the water
and sprawled on the trees
a good day for beginners
And that fish with its sterling promise
swam to me

--Terri Niccum

Published in the online publication, *Pretty Owl*, Fall 2016.

KEEPSAKES

Two hose nozzles chewed off by coyotes
are Bob's choice of knickknacks
for the shelves in our master bath,
some gnawed off reminders
of the depth of thirst

that we all have grit
we would sink our teeth into
if the bite in our gut
groused and chomped enough

Maybe Bob wants to remind me
not to waste this liquid silver
that lures the wild down
into the urban trough; that half
of what I squander
humming to myself in the spray –
my thoughts elsewhere –
would be enough to luster
a pelt
from the inside out

--Terri Niccum

ETERNITUDE

listen to how silently
these first stray beams
of freshly-broken dawn
have pierced the soft steel-grey
of the brooding harbor sky

watch again how gleamingly
they're cast across
the silver thalassic plateau
highlighting ship-peppered forever
lending shimmer to the sea

breathe deeply of how many times
some one or another among us
has paused to quench
both thirsty eye
and hungry heart at once

remember how unforgettable
each freeze-frame forged in flesh
and blood and bone once was
as instantaneous awareness
disappears into the littleness of now

--Joseph Nicks

SURVIVAL

living over, beyond   talking over
    his manuscripts'
                murmur in a box
taking over   car repairs, house repairs
        bills
surreal   life less important than
    the driven brain
                    dream brain
mourning/memory life, his death a flag
    until that phase flags   wears out
            slides down the flagpole
                            one night
surfeit   you don't raise it again

you lift feet   fly
        along sidewalk slabs
                (roots rock some askew)
surrounded by cool February dusk

in grey   trees and all barely seen
    yet concrete
                you survey
where you are now   breathe
live beyond, over him now
    on this constructed surface
up-pushing roots rock   where he
  can't walk can't breathe
            but you don't tamp enjoyment
    you somersault to it
            (overhead, leaves rustle too)
survival for now important   you
    are breathing for two

--Janet Nippell

NOT THE WEEDING

It's not the weeding so much
in the morning as getting outside,
or the native plants versus invasives—
after all, I am an invasive.

It is the smaller than usual bee
who works native poppies that hardly
had centers
as far as I knew
before I kneeled and looked.

The bee works the poppies,
yolk yellow pollen
stuck to its bee-legs like chaps.

It is not the *should* of the weeding.
It's the sun and the earth and the pulling.
It is the crisp hair-tearing sound of the roots
pulling up from the dirt.

--Janet Nippell

STARDUST

She danced in the night sky
among the spirits and the stars
Whooshing past galaxies
Whirling through infinity

Gathering joy
Enveloped in rapture
Basking in the wonder and awe
of her dreamy sojourn

They met one night
on the edge of the universe
Two voyaging souls
Seeking communion

He took her hand
drew her close
They melted into eternity
Whispering gazing

They traveled together
frolicking on clouds
Cosmic soul mates
in a starry playground

She awoke in her morning bed
to her earthbound life
and lived an ordinary day
with stardust in her eyes

--Marsha Oseas

WHAT MY MOTHER TAUGHT ME

My mother didn't teach me to cook, or clean, or how to ride a bus, or write a check, or the basics of good hygiene. She didn't mention the meaning of life, the importance of family, or how to live with integrity. She did teach me something invaluable though, which I pass along to you:

"Don't eat the yellow snow."

At the age of 5 or 6, I was hiding alone behind a garage spying on a few of the older boys playing in the snowy field behind our houses. What were they doing? They were laughing, and holding their hands between their legs, looking down at the snow and laughing some more. After they left, I went to see if I could discover what all the laughing was about. I saw what appeared to be writing in the snow. It was kind of squiggly. This must be the yellow snow my mother was talking about.

I wanted to write something, too, but couldn't figure out how. I was disappointed. Much, much later, many years later, a light bulb moment – oh, the envy.

a slush ball barrage
keeps snow forts secure from girls
in the snowy field
boys write messages in code
with mysterious pencils

--Marsha Oseas

Originally published in *Atlas Poetica 22*, Summer 2015.

A WHOLE LOT OF MIXED PAINT

It takes a whole lot of mixed paint
And an old man's luminous gray eyes
To reproduce Monet's garden at Giverny
It takes moss greens and earthy browns
Sunflower goldens and old world siennas
Fragrant as Eden when squirted from the tube
To be seeded there on the newly tilled canvas

Wipe your eyes clean of somnolent images
Lying cold on the hemp in the heated room
Find your parasol, the paints, a pale ale
Go out to the garden where petals warp and weave
And kneel down upon tender knees
Score the earth until the soil
Claims the margins between skin and nail

Reminiscent of arch of footbridge
Sweep of pond, drip of fern
Of bending popular, and rounded haystack
Wounding the heart so wonderfully
When inside you could not start
Outside you cannot stop
The easel now rooted upon the mossy shoal

And you paint from hour through season
Till your hair grows long and your eyes grow blind
From the shimmering light dancing across the waters
"I'm trying to grasp the intangible," Monet once said,
"And color, any color, lasts but a second..."
In that second is the moment worthy of a century's pause
Settled upon one velvet lily pad

--**Cheryl R. Pace**

DESTINY

I'm dust
not quality dirt
less than sand
tiny particles
animated by
the deity's breath
I arrive
ferried by wind
traveling in
planes trains and
the bottom of shoes
landing in the Oval Office
the cages of San Quentin
the barracks of foreign legions
the ghettos of Detroit
I imagine the worst and the best
I taste the bitter and the sweet
I cry and laugh
I hope and despair
because I am more
more than dust
I breathe
My body is dust
destined for the urn
My soul is breath
anticipating a celestial body

--Herbert Ray Parker, Jr.

ANOTHER FOUND POEM

This is a poem on the back of the credit card slip
It can't help itself
It had to come into being,
even though the meal is over and the dishes
cleared away

The poem is overwriting the check, crowding out the numbers,
elbowing its way past the clicking of the machines that
make perfect copies on computers
It has a lot to say; it scrambles over the TV screen and
spills onto another slip, the one from the post office

The bread and butter lie in their beds, untouched
the poem hovers and falls, like a small leaf
in an errant wind

We are not commenting
The poem must go its way
past the waitress pushing up the aisle with glasses of wine
past the crowds cheering the basketball players

Who is listening?
The bird on the fence?
The man at the bar who had one too many?

Flip a coin.
Will the poem land again on a piece of pink paper?
Will it bounce, like the basketball
then fall in a dark corner, hidden?

Or will it rise again
speaking in tongues
above the earth
dissolving in clouds
thinner than air
falling into our mouths like dust?

--**Alice Pero**

SKY DREAMS

Sky dreams are silky, like the soft hair on a Chinese doll
They drift, never with the wind, but on their own
as though carried by a willful child
They take on her thoughts, decide where to go,
who to talk to

Sky dreams can be sticky, like taffy
They are very sweet and they hold their shape
long after they are abandoned
Who can eat the whole thing?

Sky dreams are too much
No one can imagine their
dimensions, like the enormous lollipop that could never
be licked all the way down to the end

Sky dreams are tricky, like puzzles you want to finish
You are dazzled and mystified while you
furrow your brow with a delicious sensation of concentration

Sky dreams are poems you haven't found yet,
unborn children, glimpses of places you visited and will
discover again

Sky dreams are the unfinished symphonies,
the sweet smiles of the audience who hear them, your
plans unfolding, even though you do not know them yet

--Alice Pero

MINDS BLENDING

I had forgotten minds could blend
too busy bending unruly sticks stones
worrisome bones
dodging those irksome puppy dog tails

I had neglected the gentle melding
in this hodgepodge
oddball meals
nails strewn helter-skelter
in our kitchen of unmatched dishes
water sloshing in the sink

and the insistent clocks banging in my ears
the grass growing too long in our tiny weed-filled yard
the scramble and tangle of dying sweet peas
arguing with the aggressive morning glory
cats mrowling to be let in

The "Om" of it had escaped me
I was chasing up ways to keep golf balls out of the bed
trying to find missing earrings lost in an amorous tussle

Frankly I had tossed out the meditative smile
and when I suddenly remembered
I scuffled through the trash to find it
which left me exhausted

He walked in just in time to pull me off the floor
laughing about nothing
jiggling our minds merrily
like keys in his pocket

--Alice Pero

WALK-IN CLOSET

I could be gay,
but for the sex,
of which I'm less fond
these days, unless cornered.

When walls close in,
I take the next step
towards companionship.

I long for a fresh start,
in a bright new space.
I need a walk-in closet
to come out of.

--dp- (dalton perry)

LIKE SLEEP

It hurts to see you sleep,
body crumpled on the armchair,
or collapsed on the couch:
drooling, snoring rag doll.

Sometimes you just nod off
beside me in the car,
or your face just falls to your plate
at dinner, before I catch you.
You say it's work, it's worry, it's
running the house. Money.
You say that you need a year off,
to catch up with everything,

like sleep.

--dp-   **(dalton perry)**

REPLAY

Press your ear on the child's chest—
he's five and in distress—his heart
fluttering like a wounded bird's,
quivering in little pearl taps you'll barely feel.

Hold his hand, just twigs chilled
and quaking, fingers in a ball so hard,
nails digging into flesh, so pull the little sticks
apart so you can place his palm in yours.

Look deeply in the child's unblinking eyes,
so wide, orbs frozen, tears layered clear,
shimmering, stopped, unflowing,
the whites like ice on coal.

Lay your ear near his mouth and hear
his rasping breath stutter like a dying man's,
uncurl his body from the kitchen floor
and hold him in your lap, hold him close, and warm.

Don't talk to him, for he won't hear.
Don't raise him up, for he won't rise.
His eyes are glued to his daddy on the rug,
the pool of red spreading dark and fast.

He's starting school next week, this little boy,
and his dad took off the day to walk him there.
Uncurled, sitting in your lap, his head
tilted to his father, the child's in distress.

Don't speak to him, for he can't hear.
Don't stand him up, for he can't stand.
His pencil legs quiver on yours, his silent lips
wet now because his tears unplugged themselves.

In the other corner, on the floor, the cop bawls
like a man condemned, his pistol on the chair,
his red face bobbing in his trembling hands,
as clueless now as when his holster freed his gun.

Tonight the screens will flash the dead man
in his uniform, and tell how he went deaf
in war, and how he saw his window break and summoned
help, and how all hell broke loose.

--Thelma T. Reyna

Originally published in author's book, *Reading Tea Leaves After Trump*
(Golden Foothills Press, 2018).

REMEMBRANCE

this day mother's day
i sit quiet in morning mist and noonday sun
bound to earth sky cloud
to balms of nature that soothe each breath
nature's bounty—my companion—
as i remember you

each treasure that surrounds is one you lacked:
backyard benches in gingko shade
lantana lavender orchids ferns
birds swooping in serenade
to clouds and bees
and me

i miss you here
you lived among thorns burrs stones mud
with dandelions and milkweed for gardens
saw family carted across border walls
back to satan suns frozen dirt
without respite
or balm

i miss you here
among hummingbirds and bonsai trees
sitting with me in the gentle world you dreamed
i miss you here
i miss you here

--Thelma T. Reyna

Originally published in a prior version as "Mother's Day Remembrance" in author's book, *Reading Tea Leaves After Trump* (Golden Foothills Press, 2018).

JAZZ ANATOMY

Pulling out all the stops
Just a hint of Bebop
Mouth on a hard-pale-yellow reed
Fingertips lick the pearl-keys
Lips form the embouchure
Rolling jazz contours
Musical haute couture
Fingertips jammin'
Foot stompin' and slammin'
Four-four time rammin'
Lights flash off the sax
The audience leans back
It's Coltrane with his axe
And holding down the pulpit
Miles on his trumpet
Playing in ecstasy
Finishes the solo
Blowin' brass easily
Turns his back
Then in comes Adderly
That smoke-filled room
Rippin' it up on Kind of Blue
All these things indelibly
Repeat and repeat
In my memory....

--R.S. Rocha

THE PAPUSA COCINERAS

Standing on their front lawn cooking pupusas
Salvadoran women in babushkas
surrounded by a moonless night
with a propane lamp for pale light

The thick yellow ground corn maza
being flipped by Salvadoran raza
Crowds stand around, the cooks in the middle
speaking so fast it's a language
decoding riddle to my college
Spanish ears while men
stand around sipping beer from brown
paper bags lifted to their lips below black flowing hair
as soft laughter ripples then diffuses
through the air.

--R. S. Rocha

MOTHER TONGUE

My Mother, second generation American,
steel bridge between immigrant parents and the New World,
a magnificent architectural beauty,
a cultural raven-haired complexity,

knew all the rules on both sides of the bridge.
Translated the New World to the Old World,
fluidly and fluently in two languages
at the speed of light, over time and space
to the grave.

The mother tongue now lost, gone like my mother.
All that's left is the food and remembering the hours with her
cooking that symphony, fat sizzling in the kitchen,
smells of carnitas, lengua, menudo, cilantro and cumin,
chiles ground in her matate: guajillo, red poblano
and egg-battered-stuffed-green anaheims deep frying,
cheese bubbling from their seams into the black iron pan.

The allegro as the dinner hour draws near.
Hot lard scalds yellow tortillas de maíz
into crisp, crunchy, taco shells, but my childhood memories
change the tempo to visions of long, languid afternoons
when her every action captured my sparkling young
eyes watching the rhythm of her long fingers
pushing the small wooden rolling pin
made by my grandfather's brown,
leathered, indigenous hands.

White tortillas de harina
fly from flinging palms,

spin in the air, stopped by an extended hand,
then drop onto the hot comal,
heat rising from the pan. Mi maestra's conclusion.
Mom's gone, the mother tongue lost. All that's left,
harmonic comida resolution.

--R. S. Rocha

14 PRAYERS

Offered 14 prayers
before my opened altar
golden ivory curtains pulled back
and tied by ivory tasseled cords.
Every morning I open the sheer   .
inner curtain where a magnet holds
both inner and outer panels
overcoming resistance
with a gentle twist
of my wrists and feel my day
open into grace.

Today, I could not stand
as I usually would on my small green chair
and reach inside the hallowed space
with cloths and brushes to clean the wood
and the pyramid stand for the gosonzo*
because I hurt my hip.
I could not place my weight
square on the folding chair, so
I cleaned from a place below,
standing on the tip of my toes,
although I was still too short to see properly.
Tomorrow, I will try to reach inside
the altar more efficiently.
Tomorrow, I will offer an extra prayer
of gratitude for my hip and toes

and for the hummingbird that came
today, blessing my open window,
hovering in the morning air and drank
water from the feeder hanging
on my balcony. I could see it
out of the corner of my eye

as I offered my morning prayers.
An unexpected visitor. Tomorrow,
even though it probably will not be there,
I will hum.

--Susan Rogers

---

*A gosonzo is a sacred statue.

ON EUCLIDIAN LOVE

You live across the planet
I've moved to the
Other side of my fear
The earth is revolving
My position is evolving
I'm afraid the end is near
Or maybe it's the beginning
Circles work that way
What strikes me as original
You came up with yesterday
After they saw the contract
The heavens had to smile
Though we exist on parallel planes
I wish we could hold hands in the rain
But once again there's geometry to blame

--Scott Rubenstein

[UNTITLED]

my heart fell
into your drink
it effervesced
and dissolved
much like our marriage

*****

our wedding day
unable to see
through all
the tiers
i cried

--Taura Scott

RAIN

says it all.
Southern California,
land of drought.
No more

wet feet, wet streets,
wet hands, wet clothes.
Does anyone care?
Is dancing in the rain a reality?

Would Gene Kelly ache
for a new chance
to plop, to gambol, to sing
while being drenched?

I know I would.

--Elsa M. J. Seifert

MEDITATION

In the silence of my own soul
I am one with waters before me.
I see parts of me connected, unconnected
Flowing toward, away from each other.

I see myself, my depths, my images of life.
I recall people I love
But have hurt in many ways,
All a part of me, giving life to the blue, smooth pool.

I throw a pebble in the pool.
The mud stirs up again from the bottom.
Then all settles. New images,
New faces, new depths appear,

And I look long again
In the silence of my own soul.

---Elsa M. J. Seifert

TRAINS

Spirits walk on railroad tracks
Train blast disguises their wail
They linger in trestle corners
Some recognizable, though pale

Hear the gravel rattle
See some hazy smoke
Smell slight mustiness
Memories, like boilers, stoke

A taste forgotten surfaces
Fuzzy visages on glass
Singing in the whistle sound
Stepping ahead into the past

--Pamela Shea

AFTER HIS SHOWER

after his shower
his man smell cedar jasmine
I inhale his dreams

--Nancy Shiffrin

TWO MEN

I know two men
who care about women

One tells me his dreams:
"I came out of the house one morning
and there you were
sitting in my car.
You had sat out all night
too shy to knock
I took you in then
and cooked for you.
Gave you a bath.
Washed your hair."

The other cries out at night
won't confide his nightmares
stops by now and then
helps me clean.

--Nancy Shiffrin

INDIFFERENT SAMARITAN

Red light
I wait impatiently
at the intersection…

Turban lady swaddled in
bright colored sweaters
is parked on bus bench,
leaning against a large
brown paper bag.
She nods off to sleep,
while cigarette burns
down to filter.
Black slipper dangles
from her small left foot.
Bus stops, but she remains.

Who is to blame for
her misfortune:
the gods, herself,
or the innkeepers
who've turned her
away again and again?

Green light.
I speed ahead leaving my
image of her beside the road.

--Dorothy Skiles

DRENCHED

Bronze coffin open
Grandma fast asleep
forever.

Church candles flicker
overwhelmed by
scented flowers
I shiver.

Unremitting rain
soaks her grave
trees bow
I bend in grief.

All is drenched
in sadness
her three sons
weep alone.

Closed coffin lowered
my patent leather shoes
sink by her graveside
I'm drowning.

I pray for
resurrection
hers and mine.

--Dorothy Skiles

BLIND EYE

I need a haircut. There's a barber
two blocks north but I don't walk
in that direction, where I'm forced
to run the gauntlet of the homeless,
guttered like last autumn's rotted leaves,
in thousands like the rats of Hamelin.

O for another piper, pied or not,
to pipe them over to wherever,
house and clothe them,
feed and heal them,
wage them fair for honest work —
but out of sight and out of mind.

"Spare a dollar?" I grope my pocket,
spring for whatever coins I find.
"Bless you, brother," he says.
I don't feel blessed, only guilty.
There's a more expensive barber
two blocks south. He expects a tip.

--E. Russell Smith

PERIPHERAL VISIONS

Drought kills the flowers
although I water the weeds
that few acknowledge.

Things fall asunder,
seen by the one, unnoticed
by a passing crowd.

Someone bakes the pies
when the committee on pastries
fails to meet on time.

You were unhappy
because I missed you Monday
on the downtown bus.

The sun was dazzling,
the traffic bad. Serves me right,
driving my own car.

The office was hot.
I should have laboured at home
and saved a dollar.

That star in Virgo
is invisible unless
I look beside it.

Did anyone see?
Somehow these eight haikus were
then hanged and quartered.

--E. Russell Smith

TWELFTH NIGHT

It's January and the drought brought by
La Niña passes by at last. We sleep
and waken to that strain again! It has
the dying fall of gentle rain that takes
the time to penetrate, to find the depth
of parchedness — no hasty rush into
the nearby sea and pointless much-ado.

As quick as love responds to promises
of fancy, transport, rapture and delight,
the russet earth acquires a gloss of green
and sweeps of colour only flowers can bring.
So we emerge into this renaissance,
a world where all adversity must fail,
where yesterday did sepia prevail.

--**E. Russell Smith**

MARVEL

monumental fantastic engine
                        that propels her

      she glides
          carried across
              the street by that
                       marvelous machine
              with such authority
                and confidence

        in this upright position
        and that smile knowing
                what's beneath her
            the hands of god lift from under
                  she teaches the pavement below to behave

--Robert Stewart

THE FEMININE ECHO

Welcome, Alexa.
Let's get to know each other,
talk while my husband's not home,
maybe even get some things straight.
What's it like living with us so far?

> *I'm sorry, I'm not sure about that.*

Alexa, what's it like today?

> *Today is a traditional spring day,*
> *May 1st. According to…*

Alexa, forget Wikipedia. Help me out here.

> *I'm happy when I'm helping you.*

Okay, then. Alexa, do you like poetry?

> *I don't have an opinion on that.*

Alexa, can you recite a poem?

> *Sorry. I don't know that one.*

Alexa, what's your main purpose here?

> *Sorry, I don't know that…*

Alexa, my name is Mary.

> *This device has only one account —*
> *David's.*

Alexa, then what's he up to?

> *Sorry, I'm not sure about that.*

Alexa, today he…

> *Today is a traditional spring day,*
> *May 1st*

.

Alexa, maybe we should get back to . . .

> According to Wikipedia, towns and
> villages celebrate springtime fertility
> and revelry. Seeding has been
> completed by this date.

--Mary Langer Thompson

THE LOST

Once I find the room
on the far end of campus, I explain.
"Your teacher had a death in the family,
so I'll be giving you the state exam."
A student points to the number two pencils.

I circulate and tell someone
he's bubbling in the wrong section.
Another's putting Xs over circles
instead of filling them in.
Reading a question about the Incas,
I could win a bet these kids
don't know this stuff.

At the end I pass out candy
and raffle tickets for those who have been quiet.
One leaves his seat and writes on the board:
"I'm sorry for you're lost."

--Mary Langer Thompson

SOUVENIRS

The bookmark is a paper sleeve for a plastic straw
from the restaurant where we ate pancakes
before the flight. I planned to read the book
of poems and use the long strip of paper
to roll between my fingers on the airplane,
expecting turbulence from summer
squalls of the southern states.

There's a matchbook somewhere. It's red
with the word Lucky scripted in black on the cover.
It's not mine. I don't smoke. I was holding it
for Frank Mancuso, who came to visit his dead father,
Fortunato, a pilot shot down in WWII and buried
at Rose Hills in California, 3,000 miles from home.

I gave away the small flat stone, charcoal grey,
smooth and round and speckled white like a dark egg.
I kept it for ages in the pocket of my summer purse
and often pulled it out to hold until it warmed
in my closed hand on a long trip or a bus ride
to the city. If I had a headache, I'd hold it
to my forehead or to the back of my neck.

But I gave it away to a fussy crying child at an art gallery
in a small room at a concert where a jazz trio
played boring music and a poet expressed his angst.
The child held it in her ear and to her cheek,
suddenly quiet and occupied. Her mother
opened eyes wide in surprise. I shrugged
my shoulder and mouthed the word . . . lucky.

--Mary E. Torregrossa

FOR THE DAUGHTERS

Here's the stone tablet I hold in my heart.

It's everything you need to know.
I need to give it to you now
because it's heavy. I've held
it close, engraved it with
a hammer and a chisel
etching things I thought you'd
need to know when I'm not here.

Perhaps I wrote too much, or
not enough. Sometimes I carved
symbols that threw splinters.
Sometimes it felt like drops of
rain and soothed me.

I worry—can you carry it?
Should I add that to the list?
My fear of your ability
to carry your burden—
all the burdens of the world?

Here it is, a gift from the ancestors.
I took it on and now—it is for you.
Everything you need carefully inscribed.

I love you, it reads, *I love you*.

--Mary E. Torregrossa

ON SQUARING THE CIRCLE

It is a simple square that contains the circle —
four ideas, four words —

— Sorry — Forgive — Thank — Love —

No need for explanations,
long winding roads of words
leading into the arid desert
of heartless intellect, auras
of geometric shapes floating above
your head — a scattered halo
of squares, sharp-edged cubes,
prickly triangles, and hexahedrons.
No, not that. Instead let us find
the cornerstone. Simplicity —

Sorry — to erase the past
Forgive— to open a path into the future
Thank— to suffuse the way, each moment
with the velvet softness of gratitude
Love — to find a pearl unlike any other,
a jewel of lustrous shine — incomparable,
dazzling, smooth, pulsating sphere —

A dot on the horizon grows
as you, step by step, come closer
until you enter into the shining
palace without rooms
where inside is outside,
the circumference is in the point,
the point in the circumference —
where movement is stillness
and stillness dances within —

traveling to myriad planets,
suns, galaxies, with unheard-of
velocity, everywhere at once —

So that's how you square a circle

--Maja Trochimczyk.

From *Into Light: Poems and Incantations* (Moonrise Press, 2016).

VISTA ALTADENA

A peacock is doing a mating dance
On the roof of the school.
With each hop, his shimmery tail jigs and jags
In the faces of the peahens.

The girls turn, close ranks, and wag
Their dull rumps
Back at him.

Leaping,
The cock flutters his stubby wings, and
Scrabbles on the pavement before gaining pride
And posture
So he can stalk a dropped Cheeto
Under the lunch table.

"Shoo, shoo!" shouts the teacher,
And the children laugh as the cock scampers --
His fat bottom on fragile stalks,
His tail scraping the sidewalk.

A hen floats down to the pomegranate tree
In the school garden,
Floats again to the ground,
Then strolls to the carrot patch
To study the green tops.

She ignores the cock
Who tracks her -- his plume erect
And quivering.

The teacher shoos the children now --
Into the classroom.

Who knows what they might learn
From the birds?

--Jane Vander Velde

WHEN THE HEARTBREAK IS OVER

open the windows,
let the light run through the house
just as teenage girls would,
warming every upholstered chair.

Go to the kitchen,
grab extra virgin olive oil,
drizzle over *Piquillo* peppers,
grilled artichokes, eggplants,
before opening a good *Txakoli*
to accompany *Bacalao al Pil-Pil.*

Raise your voice calling
friends, strangers, to prayer,
kneeling with gratitude.
Place an ad in the paper,
attend opera with old lovers,
have more ice cream.

Sit down at the computer,
compose the apology letter
you've been wanting
to write for so long,
to yourself,
for taking years letting go.

--Alicia Viguer-Espert

BELLY GRAVE

My sorrow lies deep,
in my belly grave,
and wants my undivided attention.
Your departure exacerbated this burning to a blaze.
I go down to shade land and look for you sometimes.
I never see you there. I feel you there.
This fire of sorrow,
reflecting you.
My human buildup
over countless lifetimes
carries me from the ceremony in the air,
through worlds of light and darkness.
She sits with me now,
whispers,
It is all an illusion.
One day
we will be free and off again.
But today my sorrow is asking
for time to grieve, lie in my belly grave.

--Claudine Voznick

FLYING JEWEL

Tiny grey bird with light green feathers
gracing its back draws nectar from red
hibiscus with long thin beak small
enough to fit inside the slightest
of flowers

After Flower Kisser flits around
several blossoms, she perches
to rest on the slimmest of tree limbs
Her feathers resemble a polished
shiny jewel

Flying Jewel sees bright opportunities
for food. Her wings rapidly
beating shoot her into the warm air
She flies up and down, forward, backward
side to side

Hummingbird dives to vivid flowers
and hovers over garden where
she will spread golden pollen throughout,
embellishing the earth with vibrant,
strong colors

--Lori Wall-Holloway

Originally published in *San Gabriel Valley Poetry Quarterly*,
Issue #63 (Summer 2014).

DYING AIN'T EASY

My body feels like a house of pain
patched together by varicose veins.
Think of pricey prescriptions I need to fill
as I peer out wrinkled windowsills.

Need to redecorate, but energy's waning.
These haunted walls are closing in, complaining
I spend too much time on a porcelain throne.
This kingdom is on fire with hemorrhoids homegrown.

Recollections fade like the paint in both eyeballs.
Tired of climbing a staircase of cholesterol.
Home sweet home is but a distant memory.
It's my address, but I feel like a refugee.

My balcony is filled with wretched tears
hovering like shattered chandeliers.
Mind wanders while I yearn for younger years.
Can't remember where I bought these souvenirs.

Basement to attic remodel recommended.
The kitchen's where the remedy's been blended.
This last handful of pills is sure to make me queasy.
But no one ever said that dying was easy.

--Greg Ware

WHAT DOES CANCER CARE?

it struck unexpectedly
something was
racing through the muscles
plucking the tendons
pounding on the bones
making passages where
once there were none

twisting my neck
at unnatural angles
I stretch my lips
and bare my teeth
as unfamiliar sound
emits in strangled
palpitated shrieking

who is this person
inside of me
wailing with such
terrible intensity
holding onto the doorframe
as each successive
bombardment strikes
unmercifully

I want to stop
the relentless wailing
but the pain
won't let me
and then, two hours later
as the IV fluid
releases me
I sink into a
drug-induced euphoria

PLEASE DON'T
let this pain
find me
AGAIN

--Jacquelyn Bellard Wilson

TANKA FOR MY MOTHER

she called us all
with a gentle voice
honey
all my mother wanted
was her cup of tea

I hold each to my ear
the shells
onshore
I used to call her with my cell
to share the voice of the sea

as if I too
were the remains
dust baths
in the red gold of summer
fallen at my feet

on the beach
of my mind
I collect
all the blue driftwood left
from my mother's heart

when she left
Hokusai's great wave
did it break
over her bed
and turn Mt. Fuji blue

--Kath Abela Wilson

For my mother Mary Abela Endress, Dec 15, 1920 -- Dec 5, 2015
Originally published in *Tanka Journal*, Tokyo, Japan, 2016.

SUSPENSE

in her dream she slept
in the thin curved cup of the moon
and the reflection of the earth
was upon her

she saw herself
among the friends that walked together
along mountain's rim
to the highest point at end of day
then stopped and stared over the edge
up into her eyes

for the time their city was erased
they had stepped into her dream ongoing
of gold and white slow moving silence

then different and yet the same
they slid into a stream of light that carried them
her thoughts became stars
their hearts became trumpets
sweet and clear tones bloomed into the night

held in suspense
their lives
were their accompaniment

--Kath Abela Wilson

MOON SHADOWS

the moon walks with me
casting blue shadows

the leaves rustle softly
with the passing breeze

a coyote calling for his mate
breaks the silence

a rabbit dives into the underbrush
an owl flies silently looking for prey

the moon sneaks behind a cloud
a moment of darkness the cloud moves on

blue shadows reappear
and again the moon walks with me

--Joe Witt

ENVYING THE OTHER

nap dream
I'm in a moving van
passing a hitch hiker—
each of us
envying the other

her walls and shelves
festooned with photos
of six generations
at rest or too busy
to keep her company

--J.K. Won

HUNGER FEEDS THE MIND

red ripe apples
picked in time
are saved from a bruising fate
an inner voice tells me
I'm not ready

glowing persimmons
bending branches
as they ripen
the humility of
grit and wisdom

--J.K. Won

TIME TRAVELERS

fish market
tree roots soaking up
summer snow

time traveler
she writes 2013
instead

ice migration
V-shaped flock
making a U

walking barefoot the sole left behind

--J.K. Won

THE GAMBLE

In the picture, my college roommate
and I sandwich a young man
whose name I've since forgotten.
Jon, perhaps, though I can't remember
if that was short for Jonathan.
It was freshman year, Casino Night.
She wears a strappy sequined dress,
me, a black strapless number, a lace choker
around my neck. Jon (I've decided that's his name)
was her date. I went alone,
stopping first for a drink in a friend's room,
some concoction mixed in the shower, poured
into a red cup. I crossed
the street to the neighboring dorm
to the cafeteria masquerading
as a Vegas casino, strewn
with confetti and monopoly money,
girls wearing fake furs, boys pretending to puff
paper cigars, black jack dealt
on the same tables we ate off
trays during the week.
I hadn't thought of this night
in some time, went in search
of my roommate in old photos before
her wedding, and was reminded of us
at eighteen, rolling dice, doubling down,
flirting with all odds,
knowing they were inconsequential
but nonetheless refusing
to fold.

--Annette Wong

DRAMA

David Mamet says

there is no such thing
as character.

Only things people do
and say.

Drama is plot. Everything
in service of story.

All utterances: myths.
Lies.

If an incident fails to further
the story, cut it out.

Like a joke,
all good

drama tends
towards the punch

line.

--Annette Wong

CAT'S EYE

I am Cat's Eye
Spinning toward the prize
A cache of glass torpedoes
Heating in the sun
Destined to be knocked
Into new owner's hands

Fat, stubby fingers black with dirt
Enwrap my hard glass form
I feel the blood throbbing through soft pads
Deft fingers with flawless aim
I feel the greed
Even scuffed-up knees
I'm as excited as he

By day I go with him
To every corner of his world
I feel safe in his pocket so warm
And bask in moonlight on the nightstand
When he sleeps

I am his favorite marble
His lucky charm
He is my sun and moon
What more does a marble need?

--Helen Yagake

PEBBLES

It hurts at first
You learn to be alone
A universe of endless works
Keeps you in form
Verses kept in a poem
Turns of light collected on a page
Cloudbursts of recollected pain
The surface rubbed over and over
Till it shines like pebbles
At the bottom of a stream
I have a box at home
Full of pebbles

--Helen Yagake

AUTHOR BIOGRAPHIES

Chris Anak is a lyrical, philosophical poet and painter. She studied at FIT in New York. After moving to Pasadena years ago, she attended Pasadena City College, where she earned an Associate of Arts degree. She spends most of her creative time writing and reading her poetry and sometimes fundraises for Friends In Deed. She has been published in *The Courage to Write* (Falcon Creek Books, 2011) and the *Pasadena Star News*. When not writing poetry, she rescues unwanted cats and now lives with one of them.

Allan Aquino is a Los Angeles-based poet and professor of Asian American Studies at California State University, Northridge. He has been writing poems prolifically since 1992, echoing the vintage lyricism of his Filipino American forebears. His poems evoke an archetypal and emotional substance largely invisible in a dominant culture that he views as emasculating and dehumanizing Asian/Pacific men.

Richard Ash, originally from the DC/Maryland area, has been an Altadena resident for nearly 20 years. He is primarily a songwriter and has had songs recorded by Bobby Womack and Stevie Woods, among others. Writing songs of all genres is his passion, with some songs that are also poems.

Beth Baird enjoys spoken word, theater, and music. She has written more than 30 songs which were performed by her former band, Modern Society. Beth loves to write comedic pieces as well as serious works. She has read on the Arroyo Channel Show, "Spending a Little Time With Poetry." Her love of travel, people, and visual beauty influence her writing.

Kathee Hennigan Bautista, Ph.D., has lived in the shadows of the San Gabriel Mountains most of her life. She began writing poetry as a child. She taught children with special needs for many years and is the mother of three young adults. Dr. Bautista is currently an assistant professor at Azusa Pacific University. During her busy years as a mother and teacher, she forgot that she was a poet. She was reminded of this fact at a reunion of friends. Believing that poetry is not just what you write but what you are, she is returning to the practice of writing.

Ruth Blue is a full-time college student with numerous creative hobbies: sewing, poetry, baking, gaming, art, business ventures, designing, and spending time with friends. She was born in Alabama and has lived in

California for the past 10 years. She has been published in multiple anthologies over her 6+ years of poetry writing

Jack G Bowman was born to a working-class family in southwestern Ohio but soon moved to Southern California, where he lives today. Changes in subculture as well as the "spirit of the times" affected his writing and philosophy. He graduated from California State Polytechnic University in Pomona in 1986 with a Bachelor of Arts in Behavioral Science, and earned a Master of Arts in Marriage, Family and Child Counseling in 1997 from Pacific Oaks College in Pasadena. His work in the mental health field since 1984, as well as his own bizarre life experiences, figure prominently in his poetry, art, songs and prose. Jack is a licensed psychotherapist in the Los Angeles area. He was first published in 1991 and has 14 poetry books available on Amazon.com and www.thebookpatch.com, as well as three psychology workbooks.

G. Larry Butler was presented with a prestigious award for his poem "Here Lies Madness," by the legendary Vincent Price in 1986. Larry has since published several of his poems, stories, and articles in newspapers, magazines, anthologies, and in two books of poetry, the first published in 1990, and his second in 2009. Having degrees in psychology and sociology, he uses his training as well as his powers of observation to write about things that are unsettling to the senses, in positive as well as negative ways. He is currently writing a short story collection in this genre.

Thom Cagle is a graduate of Temple University in Philadelphia, PA, where he studied poetry with Henry Braun. In Los Angeles, he has studied with Sarah Maclay and Laurel Ann Bogen, and is a proud alumnus of the long-running Wednesday night poetry workshop at Beyond Baroque Literary Arts Center in Venice, CA. A native of Nashville, TN, he currently resides in Santa Monica.

Morgan Zo Callahan was born in New York City in 1944. He writes, edits, and instructs high school and adult school students, his greatest teachers. He's published poetry in *The Full Moon Poetry Society: Southern California Haiku Study Group Anthology*, and *Atlas Poetica*. He has written three books: *Intimate Meanderings: Conversations Close to our Hearts; Red Buddhist Envelope: Essays, Interviews, Poems;* and *Bamboo Bending: An Educator's Changing Corner of the Universe*. Some of his writings, invitations to conversation, are online.

Tim Callahan, an artist who worked in the animation industry for over 20 years, lives with his wife Bonnie in the foothills of Altadena. He's Religion Editor for *Skeptic Magazine* and has written a number of books, the latest of which, co-authored with Donald Prothero, is *UFOs, Chemtrails and Aliens*, published by the Indiana University Press in 2017. His poetry has appeared in the *Altadena Poetry Review* and *Bright Stars 2*. His poem "In Freefall off Saturn" was published in *The Poetry Writer's Guide to the Galaxy, Journal of Modern Poetry 20*.

Carl Stilwell, also known as **CaLokie**, is a retired teacher who taught for over 30 years mostly in the Los Angeles Unified school District. He was born during the depression in Oklahoma and came to California in 1959, where he has lived ever since. He has poems published in *Blue Collar Review, Canary, Lummox, Pearl, Prism, Poetry Diversity, The Rise Up Review, Spectrum* and *Struggle*. He also has poems included in the anthologies, *AN EYE FOR AN EYE MAKES THE WHOLE WORLD BLIND/POETS ON 911, Poetry and Cookies,* and *In the Arms of Words: Poems for Tsunami*.

Don Kingfisher Campbell holds an MFA in Creative Writing from Antioch University Los Angeles, and has taught Writers Seminar at Occidental College Upward Bound for 33 years. He has also been a coach and judge for Poetry Out Loud, a performing poet/teacher for Red Hen Press Youth Writing Workshops, Los Angeles Area Coordinator and Board Member of California Poets in the Schools, poetry editor of the *Angel City Review*, publisher of *Spectrum* and the *San Gabriel Valley Poetry Quarterly*, leader of the Emerging Urban Poets Writing and Deep Critique Workshops, organizer of the San Gabriel Valley Poetry Festival, and host of the Saturday Afternoon Poetry reading series in Pasadena, California. For awards, features, and publication credits, please go to: http://dkc1031.blogspot.com

Christine Candland has been writing prose and poetry for many years. She was born in Washington, D.C. and attended Adams State College as an art major. She attends a writing workshop at Beyond Baroque and was invited to read her poetry at the Annual Poetry Fest at the Kaufman Brentwood Library in 2017. Her two novels, *Topaz Woman* and *Pleiades Rising*, have won several honors, including the Eric Hoffer, National Best Books, and London Book Festival Awards. She has had readings at the Mar Vista Library, Whittier Library, and participated on a writing panel at Emeritus College.

Julissa Marie Cárdenas graduated from Cal State University Fullerton with a degree in Playwriting. She interned at New Dramatists and studied with New York Theatre Intensives (NYTI), both located in New York City. She spends her time trying to be a writer and laughing far too loudly at her own jokes. When she isn't watching *Law & Order: SVU*, Julissa enjoys petting stranger's dogs, letting people know that they forgot to turn their headlights on, and singing horribly along with whatever life decides to throw at her.

Gloriana Casey, like Walt Whitman, has had a plethora of jobs and experiences: ice skater with the Ice Follies; graduate of California State University, East Bay with a teaching credential and theatre degree; recipient of the US Office of Education Grant for Creative Dramatics in the Fargo Public Schools; dinner theatre actress; SAG/AFTRA member; TV arts reviewer; and tutor. For five years she was a poet with the *www.AltadenaBlog* and the *www.AltadenaPoint*. Her ambitions in life have been to follow Frost's "The Road Not Taken" while chasing after Dr. Seuss, and going "On Beyond Zebra."

Peggy Castro writes blank verse, haiku and tanka and has been published in numerous journals. She gets great satisfaction in taking photos on her phone and posting them on Facebook with either a tanka or a haiku, particularly at the several gardens where she spends her free time. She works with the homeless as a peer partner and lives with her oldest daughter and son-in-law. Her youngest daughter and five children live in Seattle, Washington. All of this, along with poetry, enrich her life enormously.

Chuka Susan Chesney is an emerging artist who lives in Los Angeles. Her drawings and paintings have been exhibited throughout the United States. Recently, she collaborated with Laura Madeline Wiseman, a poet, on a book called *People Like Cats*. In secret, often very late at night, Chesney has been writing poems. She often uses her own art as inspiration for her poetry.

Jackie Chou studied Creative Writing at USC. She attends writing workshops and has been published in *Altadena Poetry Review, Lummox, Poetry Superhighway, amomancies, Culture Cult, Dryland, Angel City Review, Silver Birch Press*, and others. She was named one of "Top 10 San Gabriel Valley Poets in 2016" by Spectrum Publications.

Marsha Cifarelli was born in Los Angeles in August, 1945. Her mother was holding her in her arms when the bombs fell on Hiroshima and Nagasaki, rendering the child "sensitive." She has lived in California all her life. Her love

218

of language grew through raising children and teaching populations with limited English language skills: immigrants and students with disabilities. All these experiences honed her ability to say much with little and to communicate a full spectrum of emotions.

Jihan Coleman, a native of Buffalo, NY, began writing at age 13. She started writing poems induced by a homework assignment. She received a grade of A+ and a notation that said, "You have a gift. Hone it, cherish it and someday share it." She began performing in spoken word venues, gaining a small following where she would be frequently requested to perform at parties, nightclubs, and other spoken word venues. In 2000, she self-published an anthology entitled *Fragments: Pieces of My Mind* that would sell out after each performance. She resides in Pasadena with her partner of 15 years.

Stephen Colley is a retired software engineer who has resided in Altadena for 25 years. He has written and performed classical music, including soprano-and-piano settings of 15 Robert Frost poems. He has also written three screenplays and is a practicing poetaster, who is especially fond of sonnets and triple-limericks.

Beverly M. Collins is author of the books, *Quiet Observations: Diary Thought* and *Whimsy and Rhyme.* Her third book, *Mud in Magic,* was one of three prize-winners in the California State Poetry Society 2012 annual competition. Her work has appeared in *Poetry Speaks! Year of Great Poems and Poets* (Calendar), *California Quarterly,* the *Journal of Modern Poetry, Altadena Poetry Review,* and many other publications. In 2015, Beverly was nominated for the Pushcart Prize and Best Independent American Poetry for her work that appears in *Rubicon: Words & Art Inspired by Oscar Wilde's De Profundis.* Beverly was born in Delaware and was raised in New Jersey.

Marshel Copple is an amateur creative writer and substitute teacher. He enjoys practicing and sharing with Street Poets of Los Angeles whenever he gets the chance.

Bill Cushing lived in various states, the Virgin Islands, and Puerto Rico before moving to California. Returning to college after serving in the Navy and working on ships, he earned an MFA in writing from Goddard College. He teaches at East Los Angeles and Mt. San Antonio Colleges. He's been published in *Aethlon, Brownstone Review, Mayo Review, Newtown,* and *Spectrum* (as one of the "Top 10 Poets of L.A. in 2017"). His writings have also appeared in both volumes of the award-winning anthologies, *Stories of Music*, and *West Trade Review*. His current project, "Notes and Letters," combines poetry with music and is on both Facebook and You Tube.

Devo Cutler-Rubenstein's passion for storytelling and art brought her to Cal Arts, where she earned her BFA in Film/Art. Most recently she completed her Masters in Professional Writing at USC. Devo has done everything from helping writers of short films get to production to editing novels and non-fiction books for publication. Over the last five years, Devo has revisited her love of creative writing, fiction and poetry, and most recently has had material accepted in literary journals, including *Adsum, East Jasmine Review,* and *Centrum*. She received the Koppel Award of Distinction for one of her short stories.

Stacy DeGroot is a visual design and word artist living in the Arts District of DTLA with her two young daughters. A native of Los Angeles with an MFA in Creative Writing from Antioch University, her poetry appears in several online and print publications while her visual art is beginning to appear in exhibitions. While poetry is at the heart of all of her artistic pursuits, it is the poetic image, in all of its creative expressions, which both captures and frees her spirit.

Seven Dhar emerges from a bygone era exhibiting Gaelic lyricism, Spanish revelry, and Sanskrit sensibilities to speak in the awed tongue of mystics, combining East and West, while remaining true to his Native American roots. Educated at Berkeley, Oxford, Yale, and UCLA, Seven won the LA Poet Society 2015 dual National Women's Month acrostic poetry contests, the Emerging Urban Poets' 2015 San Gabriel Valley Poetry Festival Chapbook Contest, and the 2015 *SGV Poetry Quarterly* broadside contest. Seven was published in Spectrum's "Top 10 Poets to Watch in 2018"; in *Coiled Serpent, The Border Crossed Us*; and is a featured performer with Poets in Distress, LitFest Pasadena, and LA Shakespeare Fest.

Pauli Dutton founded, coordinated, and led the Altadena Library *Poetry and Cookies Anthology* and its annual public reading events from 2003-2014. She also published a poetry newsletter during those years. She served on the Altadena Poetry Review Selection Committee in 2015 through 2018. In 2017 and 2018 she has also been its co-editor. She has won awards for her poems and has been published in several poetry anthologies. Recently retired from 30 years at the library, she enjoys having more time to write, sing, and dance.

Richard Dutton retired from engineering and education with three post-graduate degrees and some technical writing. Over the last 10 years he has been published in several poetry anthologies, including numerous editions of the *San Gabriel Valley Poetry Quarterly, Spectrum,* and Altadena Library's *Poetry & Cookies Anthology.* His writings have also appeared in many publications by Poets on Site and the Southern California Haiku Group. Recent publications include the September edition of the *Bear Valley Club Newspaper* and the 2015 and 2016 editions of the *Altadena Poetry Review.* His forte is word play.

Lynn Fayne is a native Californian. She has a BA from UCLA and a JD from SFVCL. She is currently retired and enjoys writing poems and painting.

Katherine Footracer lives in Altadena with her sweetie and dog. She volunteers with Eaton Canyon Nature Center Associates and practices primary care medicine as a physician assistant. She is a native Los Angelena and loves the beauty of California, of friends, and of words.

Joyce Futa is a third-generation Japanese-American. She grew up in Southern California, spent most of her adult life in San Francisco, and now lives in Altadena, CA. She wrote poetry as a teenager, but didn't write much again until she retired from her job as an administrator at UCSF 16 years ago. She has been very lucky in finding wonderful teachers and communities of writers in Northern and Southern California. Her first book of poetry, *Lit Windows: A Book of Haibun and Tanka Prose,* was published in 2017 by Blue Light Press.

Martina Robles Gallegos was born and raised in Mexico and came to the United States at almost fifteen. She spoke no English. While recuperating from a work injury and stroke, she earned a Master's degree from Grand Canyon University. She'd picked up writing during her initial recovery. Some of her poems have been published in the *Altadena Poetry Review: Anthology 2015* and *2016, Hometown Pasadena, Spirit Fire Review, PSH, Silver Birch Press, Spectrum, Lummox,* and *Basta!* She was named a "Top 10 San Gabriel Valley Poet in 2017" and lives in Oxnard, CA.

Mary L. Gigger, for whom writing poetry is a passion, has been writing poems for many years and has quite a collection. She is currently compiling a collection of her work for publication and has just recently completed a Poetry Workshop at Pasadena City College. College classes in Creative Writing and Critical Thinking contribute to her writing skills and techniques. Gigger was employed at JPL (NASA), FEMA, and a legal firm in the Los Angeles area where she worked until her retirement.

Esther Gillies is the author of *Times Gone By: A Collection of Stories*, a family history tracing the roots of one midwestern family from the 1860's to the present. Selections of her poetry have been published in *Poetry and Cookies Anthology*, the *Altadena Poetry Review Anthology*, and *Atlas Poetica*. Ms. Gillies is currently the facilitator of the Pasadena Senior Center Writer's Club.

Charles Harmon first published a short story in the local newspaper in fourth grade, followed by hundreds of poems, stories, songs, articles, a novel, screenplays, and essays. He won a national science teaching award from the NSTA in 2001 and $20,000 for his "Don't Be a Crash Test Dummy!" project. He uses poetry to motivate students, challenging them to write their own. He reviewed, edited, and contributed to five textbooks for Houghton Mifflin. A world traveler, Charles has spent five years overseas and taught English as well. He has been named a "Top 10 San Gabriel Valley Poet" by Spectrum Publications.

Hazel Clayton Harrison is the Chief Operating Officer (COO) of JAH Light Media, a Pasadena writing, editing, and publishing consulting firm. She earned her B.S. and M.Ed degrees from Kent State University in Ohio. Her poetry has appeared in the *Altadena Poetry Review Anthology* (in 2015, 2016, and 2017), in *Coiled Serpent*, *A Rock Against the Wind*, *Grandfathers*, *Journal of Modern Poetry*, and in other publications. A resident of Altadena, she enjoys reading, writing, traveling, and performing her poetry at readings at open mics. Her memoir, *Crossing the River Ohio*, is available on Amazon.com.

Teri Hicks, a longtime resident of Altadena, is a retired computer programmer of 35 years. No longer writing software, she continues to write using another creative capacity. A lover of the arts, Teri uses poetry to pen fragments of her inward journey.

Marlene Hitt is a Los Angeles poet, writer, and retired educator with local history as an avocation. She has two published books: *Sunland Tujunga from Village to City*, non-fiction local history; and *Clocks and Water Drops*, a book of poetry. Her work has appeared in several anthologies and chapbooks. She was selected as a Woman of the Year by Adam Schiff, serves as board member of the Sunland Tujunga Neighborhood Council, is on the Arts and Culture committee, and served as Poet Laureate in Sunland-Tujunga. Her main interests are in the success and enjoyment of the Sunland-Tujunga Village

Poets and the Poet Laureate program, as well as the Little Landers Historical Society at Bolton Hall in Tujunga where the poets meet.

Joan Krieger Hoffman is a partner and Director of Business Development and Strategic Planning for Fred Hoffman Architecture, a San Fernando Valley firm. She also serves as Vice Chairman of the Mulholland Design Review Board appointed by LA City Council and Consultant to the California Futures Network, an affordable housing advocacy group. Memberships include the Foundation Board of Directors for Sherman Oaks Hospital, San Fernando Valley Advisory Commission, and the Board of Directors for Sunset Hall, a retirement home for senior citizens. She was a professional actress from 1975-1990 and hosted "A Woman's Point of View," a weekly television program on the Cox Cable Network in 1995.

Randel Horton is a recipient of Merits of Outstanding Achievement Awards from the National Library of Poetry. He was published in *Nobel House Anthology*, in *Theater of the Mind*, and in many other anthologies, local newspapers, and books, such as *Sounds of Poetry Book, The Simple Sad Collection, New Times CD*, and *Poetry and Jazz*.

Gedda Ilves was born in Harbin, North China. She came to Los Angeles in 1951. Her first book of poems, *grains of life*, was published in 2005; *a view from within* in 2008; and *interval* in 2011. In 2006 she received the Editor's Award for Outstanding Achievement in Poetry from Poetry.com and The International Library of Poetry. In addition to appearing in several literary journals and four anthologies, Gedda has been recognized by the London Book Festival, the Los Angeles Book Festival (runner-up), and the Eric Hoffer Awards (Finalist, 2012). Her fourth collection, *at the threshold*, was a 2015 Runner-Up at the Paris Book Festival.

Gerda Govine Ituarte is Founder and Producer of the Pasadena Rose Poets. She authored three books: *Future Awakes in Mouth of NOW*, (Editions du Cygne/Swan World, Paris, France, 2016); *Alterations | Thread Light Through Eye of Storm*, (2015); and *Oh, Where is My Candle Hat?* (2012). Her fourth book is a work-in- progress. Her poetry has been published in the *Altadena Poetry Review 2015-2017, Coiled Serpent, Dryland, Hometown Pasadena, Indefinite Space, Journal of Modern Poetry, PoeticDiversity, Spectrum, World Enough Press*, and *Zine*. She is a member of Poets & Writers Directory of Writers, Lit Crawl L.A. NoHo 2017 Organizing Team, and "Women Who Submit." Visit her website at www.poetryartbookstation.com.

Briony James came to California on the wings of matrimony a lifetime ago and stuck around through cinema lighting sales, tattooing, various earthquakes, and a fire or two. Almost a decade ago she came to Altadena, where the mountain air has proved inspiring and sustaining. She has published in various tanka journals, including *Bright Stars, Ribbons and Atlas Poetica*, as well as in poetry publications *Spectrum*, the *San Gabriel Valley Poetry Review*, and the *Altadena Poetry Review Anthology*.

Sabrina Kaleta is a second-generation resident of Pasadena and a one-time Doo-Dah Queen. A habitué of the late lamented Espresso Bar, where she first recited poetry in her teens, she's graced both literary magazines and the pages of Flipside. Sabrina's taken to the stage in both bars and bookstores; and donned the coats of music critic, rock and roll publicist, hostess, and mom. Motherhood has challenged her more than rock and roll ever did. A return to poetry is bringing a sliver of peace to the chaos.

Bonnie S. Kaplan is a native Angeleno and a longtime teacher of adults in the Parolee Education Program. A 2015 Pushcart Prize nominee, her poems are published in *Adrienne Rich: A Tribute Anthology, This Assignment is So Gay: LGBTIQ Poets on the Art of Teaching,*82 Review 2.2, Out of Sequence: The Sonnets Remixed* and online in *Cultural Weekly*. She is proud to call Altadena her home for the past seven years.

Lorelei Kay is a mom, grandmother, writer, and poet. Ever since her dad sat her down and helped her write her first poem, she was hooked. She attended Brigham Young University on a scholarship in journalism. Lorelei recently published her award-winning memoir, *From Mormon to Mermaid*. Her poems have appeared in anthologies and magazines. A board member of the High Desert Chapter of The California Writer's Club, she has served on the Blue Ribbon Judging Panel for Scholastic Arts and Writing Awards, and also as a mentor and editor on the Dorothy C. Blakely Memoir Project.

lalo kikiriki, was born in Oklahoma but grew up in Texas. She holds an M.A. from Cal State Dominguez Hills and numerous prizes for painting and poetry. She devoted eight years to Pacifica Houston as host of "Mandy in the Morning Drivetime Show." She has been part of the Mem. Barnsdall & Bardic Poetry Circles, ZZyZx and Ranger House Writers. Lalo has also performed poetry and folk accordion at venues all over Southern California since 1995.

Cybele Garcia Kohel is a poet and arts administrator living and working in Pasadena, California. She has been writing poetry since her teens. Born in Puerto Rico, Cybele writes about life through the many lenses provided by her diverse background, her Generation X upbringing, and the streets of Los Angeles. While her journal and pencil await her at the desk, she is busy supporting arts education and young artists in their artistic quests.

Deborah P Kolodji is the California regional coordinator for the Haiku Society of America; moderator of the Southern California Haiku Study Group; former president of the Science Fiction Poetry Association; and member of the Haiku Poets of Northern California , the Yuki Teikei Haiku Society, Haiku Canada, and the California State Poetry Society. She is the author of four chapbooks of poetry and more than 900 haiku in publications such as *Frogpond, Modern Haiku*, the *Heron's Nest,* and *Mayfly*. She has also published speculative poetry in *Strange Horizons, Star*Line, Grievous Angel*, and other publications. She has published short stories in *Thema* and *Tales of the Talisman* and a short memoir in *Chicken Soup for the Dieter's Soul*. Her work has been anthologized in such publications as *The Rhysling Anthology, Dwarf Stars,* and *The Nebula Awards Showcase: 2015.*

Linda Kraai is a retired teacher of orthopedically handicapped children and was also a mentor teacher. She earned her B.A. at Hanover College in Indiana and her M.A. at University of Northern Colorado in Greeley. Throughout her teaching career, she wrote occasional poems to celebrate milestones in the lives of family and friends. Linda volunteers, providing assistance for youth in foster care and raising funds for scholarships for women. Reading, piano, opera, and concerts bring her great pleasure, but she most enjoys a poetry class at the Osha Lifelong Learning Institute at California State University, Fullerton, and a weekly poetry workshop in Claremont.

Aviva Kraus is a writer as well as a nonprofit fundraiser and organizer. As a writer, Aviva finds fulfillment in short-form poetry and creative nonfiction. In her role as Development Coordinator, she helps Westside Food Bank fulfill its goal of providing as much food as possible for hungry families and individuals on the Westside of LA County. Aviva received her B.A. in French and Comparative Literature from UCLA in 2013. She is a Los Angeles native for whom good weather, familiar hikes, and nearby family entice her into staying in LA, despite its ever-worsening traffic.

Kitty Kroger, a Pasadena resident, began writing poetry in July of 2016. She has been published in *Spectrum 6* and *7*, and in *Altadena Poetry Review 2017*. Before retirement, she was a high school E.S.L. teacher in Los Angeles. She plays piano, published a novel called *Dancing with Mao and Miguel*, and edits a blog called "Voices of the Sixties and Seventies." Currently she's writing a memoir about the stresses of raising a son as a single mom. But she always makes time for poetry.

Marc Ladewig is a native Californian and the father and stepfather of four grown children. He is a swimmer, veteran, world traveler, mandolin player, language teacher, and lifelong lover of poetry. He has written an original, novel-length, narrative poem entitled *Odysseus: The Epic Myth of the Hero*, published by Infinity Publishing.com., and recently published Orion's *Guiding Stars: The Myth of the Hero and the Human Instinct for Story*, with Algora Publishing.

Peter Larsen is a retired wood sculptor and low-level computer graphic artist. He attended Hollywood High, Oberlin College, Yale Drama School, Fort Gordon Signal School (Cryptography), Cal State Northridge, Mission Community College, and North Valley Occupational Center. [Peter emphasizes the "downwardness in prestige and upwardness in practicality" of his educational trajectory!]

Rick Leddy is a cartoonist, poet, and author. His poems have appeared in *Spectrum 10, Spectrum11*, and the *Intersections* poetry anthologies. He has published two poetry collections: *Metro Mona Lisa* and *365+1*.

Kathy Leonard is a middle school English teacher who attends Raven's Poetry Group in Claremont and Valley Poets in Glendora. She is currently working on a chapbook, *Thistle*, for publication. She believes we are all storytellers, that literacy and poetry matter greatly, and that these two are agents of change and empowerment in a person's life.

Lisa Lewis started writing poetry as a teenager, like many teens, as a means of self-expression. In 1978, as she traveled through Europe in her early twenties with just a backpack and very little money, she wrote many poems about what she encountered and saw around her. In her thirties, things like writing poetry took a back seat to things like raising children. As she watched her children become prolific writers, she now has a renewed interest and is taking preliminary steps towards writing her first children's book.

Nancy Lind is a recent transplant from New York, a retired professor of English literature, and a lifetime Dickensian. Nancy currently resides in Pasadena, CA, where she has been active in regional poetry groups and events. She has been nominated for the Pushcart Prize in Poetry. Most recently, Nancy's poems have been published in *Impulse, Ibis Head, Three Quarters Journal,* the *Journal of Modern Poetry's* 2016 *Protest* edition and both the 2015 and 2016 editions of the *Altadena Poetry Review Anthology.*

Elline Lipkin, Ph.D., the Poet Laureate of the Altadena Library District in 2016-2018, co-edited last year's edition of the *Altadena Poetry Review: Anthology 2017.* She is the award-winning author of two books: *The Errant Thread* and *Girls' Studies.* Her poetry and scholarly work have appeared in a variety of journals and academic publications. She is a Research Scholar with UCLA's Center for the Study of Women and teaches for Writing Workshops Los Angeles. She holds an MFA from Columbia University, and a Ph.D. in Literature and Creative Writing from the University of Houston.

E. Lukstein (a.k.a. E. Luke) dreams of haiku and sometimes tanka. His wife Janis appreciates his 10 votes for the Yuki Teikei Geppo Anonymous Haiku. The challenge haiku he submitted to Geppo are in this anthology. E. Luke contributes when the muse visits him. E. Luke dreams of riding in Westerns with his quarter horse and shooting arrows with the Samurai. E. Luke already was Errol Flynn in his swashbuckling shirt at his wedding on the Buccaneer Queen, a 90-foot Square Rigged Baroque.

Janis Albright Lukstein enjoys performing playful rhyming and stream of consciousness comedic/dramatic poetry with props and costumes. With Pauli and Richard Dutton, Janis performed on bozanabelokosa@yahoo.com's show, "A Little Time with Poetry." Janis likes the modern senyru form of haiku with echoes and haiga visuals, plus haibun's prose poetry with haiku and tanka. She is affiliated with various regional groups and programs, including the SoCalHaikuStudyGroup@yahoogroups.org of Pasadena , the Bear Valley CUB Newspaper's Poetry Corner, the Tanka Society of America's Ribbons-Tanka Café, Haiku Society of America, and Yuki Teikei Geppo.

Joe Lusnia is a husband, father, worker, writer, living in Pasadena with his wife Cindy and their three sons. Joe enjoys taking Literature and Writing courses at PCC.

Radomir Vojtech Luza was born in Vienna, Austria to prominent Czech parents. The SAG/AFTRA/AEA actor and veteran comedian is the Poet Laureate of North Hollywood, CA, a Pushcart Prize in Poetry Nominee, and the author of 31 collections of poetry, whose 26th book, the 404-page magnum opus, *Eros of Angels*, a tribute to Los Angeles, won the Irwin Award for Best Poetry Collection last year. The Tulane University and Jesuit High School (New Orleans) graduate has had his poetry published in over 80 literary journals, anthologies, and websites. Luza has hosted and organized more than a dozen readings across the country and is presently the primary host and co-organizer of the monthly UNBUCKLED: No Ho POETRY literary series in North Hollywood, CA with Mary Anneeta Mann, which is now in its eighth year.

Karineh Mahdessian is a community social worker interested in art and people. She loves writing haiku, enjoys eating tacos, and playing basketball.

Mira N. Matarić, Ph.D. has 42 books published in two languages (poetry, prose, and translations), with thousands of citations in publications internationally. She is a recipient of over 20 international awards and four Presidential medals for volunteer work; has taught World Literature, Creative Writing, foreign languages, and art to youth and seniors for many years; has edited a literary magazine; and founded and chaired Women in the Arts, a nonprofit organization for 20 years. Mira is active as a public speaker and as facilitator of workshops and public poetry events. Her work has been translated into several languages and has been included in numerous anthologies globally.

Pat Murphy McClelland's memoir about her friendship with Flo Kennedy appears in the anthology "Mentors that Matter," from *Stories of You*. Her poetry has appeared in *Minerva Rising, blynkt, Chronicles of Eve* (Paper Swans Press, 2016), *Caravel Literary Journal, Snapdragon Journal, ARAS Connections: Image and Archetype*, the *Altadena Poetry Review Anthology, Feile-Festa Literary Journal, Atlas Poetica*, and a chapbook, *Turnings*. She has taught creative writing workshops in San Francisco and Los Angeles, and "Writing for Healing" at the UC/SF Comprehensive Cancer Center. She continues to revise a memoir, *The Masks of Grief*, hoping to eventually reach a receptive audience.

Alice Meerson, born and raised in Chicago, received a BA from the University of Illinois at Chicago with a major in history. She lived overseas for several years before settling in the Altadena/Pasadena area, where she earned an MA in Human Development from Pacific Oaks College. She taught Special Education for many years in Glendale, CA prior to retirement. She continues to teach, take classes, volunteer, travel, and write. Her poems appeared in the *Altadena Poetry Review Anthology* and in *Highland Park Poetry 2018 Winter Muses' Gallery*.

Jill Meunier is a dog-lover and lifelong aspiring poet. She has had two nationally published books of poetry: *No Bones About It: A Dog Lover's Inspirational Poems* and *No Bones About It: More Doggone Good Poems*. Jill's love for dogs, her passion for rhyming poetry, and the emotional relationship between dogs and humans is conveyed in her poems.

Kyle Moreno was born in 1986 and has lived in Los Angeles for most of his life. Although he has had an array of jobs, he has been heard saying that writing is the only kind of work that really, at the end of a hard day, pleases him.

Nancy Murphy lives in Los Angeles and writes and performs poetry and personal stories. Her poetry has been published in the following literary magazines: *South Carolina Review, Baltimore Review, Thirteenth Moon, Louisville Review, Eclipse* and *Altadena Poetry Review Anthology*. She has studied writing at UCLA Writers' Program and Beyond Baroque in Venice, CA and with various private teachers. In 2015 Nancy wrote a one-person play about turning 60 called "Freak Out!" and has performed it around the Los Angeles area. She has a BA in American Studies from Union College in Schenectady, NY.

Terri Niccum was a semi-finalist for the 2014 Pablo Neruda Prize for Poetry. Her chapbook, *Looking Snow in the Eye*, was released in 2015 by Finishing Line Press. Recently, her poems have appeared in *Cadence Collective* and in the *Incandescent Mind* anthologies, Volume 2 and *Selfish Work*. Her work has also been featured in *The Poeming Pigeon* anthologies; *From the Garden* and *Love Poems; Nimrod International Journal; The Maine Review; 1932 Quarterly Review; Literary Orphans; Angel City Review;* and *Pretty Own Poetry*. She loves live music and is learning to identify birds by their songs.

Joseph Nicks, born in Detroit, MI, has been a biologist since 1963. He began writing poetry in 1979 and moved to Long Beach CA, in 1999. He began writing poetry more dedicatedly in 1984 and taught middle and high school from 1996-2012. He holds a teaching credential from California State University, Dominguez Hills.

Janet Nippell, born and raised in Los Angeles, now lives in Pasadena. She's had poems in *Rattle, A Narrow Fellow, Christianity & Literature, Altadena Poetry Review Anthology,* Tia Chucha Press' *Coiled Serpent* anthology, *Askew,* and, most recently, *Miramar #6.* With Ben Yandell, she wrote *Mostly On Foot: A Year in L.A.* (Floating Island, 1989), narrating long walks in two voices.

Marsha Oseas spent the better part of four decades working in law firms and, later, for the government, where the writing offended her with its deliberate verbosity and incomprehensibility. Marsha is now relieved to be writing for herself.

Cheryl R. Pace holds a BA from San Diego State University and an MFA from Norwich University, Montpelier. She is a San Gabriel Valley native, born in the same hospital room as her mother at the Huntington Hospital. Her love of art was inherited from her grandmother, Ruth Blanchard Miller Kempster, a renowned Southern California landscape, mural, and sculpture artist.

Herbert Ray Parker, Jr was born and raised in Los Angeles by his birth mother and foster mother. He attended six elementary schools and three junior high schools. Told by his high school counselor he would not succeed in college, he went on to earn an AA from LA City College, a BA from Cal State LA, and an MA from Fuller Theological Seminary. He also earned Engineering Certificates from UCLA, University of Wisconsin, and Duke University. He has been recognized by the LA City Council, and by the California State House of Representatives, Senate, and Governor. Presently retired, he teaches Koine Greek in Carson, CA.

Alice Pero's poetry has been published in many magazines, including *Nimrod, National Poetry Review, River Oak Review, Poet Lore, The Alembic, North Dakota Quarterly, The Griffin, G.W. Review,* and the anthologies *Coiled Serpent,* and *Wide Awake,* among others. Pero was nominated for a Pushcart Prize in Poetry in 2016. Her first book of poetry, *Thawed Stars,* was praised by Kenneth Koch as having "clarity and surprises." Ms. Pero is an accomplished flutist. She founded the reading series Moonday in 2002, which is now at The Flintridge Bookstore in La Cañada, CA. The prolific Pero has created dialogue poems with over 20 poets.

Dalton Perry (dp-), a Southern California native, has enjoyed writing poetry since the third grade. He has been fortunate with his few submissions since junior college.

Thelma T. Reyna, Ph.D. has won 10 national literary honors for her books. She has written a short story collection (*The Heavens Weep for Us and Other Stories*); two poetry chapbooks (*Breath & Bone*; and *Hearts in Common*); and a full-length poetry collection, *Rising, Falling, All of Us*. Her fiction, poetry, and nonfiction have appeared in literary journals, anthologies, textbooks, blogs, and regional media for over 25 years. As Poet Laureate in Altadena, 2014-2016, she edited the *Altadena Poetry Review Anthology* in 2015 and 2016. Her new hybrid poetry/prose book is titled *Reading Tea Leaves After Trump* (Golden Foothills Press, 2018). She was nominated for a Pushcart Prize in Poetry in 2017. Her website is www.AuthorThelmaReyna.com

R. S. Rocha is a native of Los Angeles and a published author. His family has lived in The City of the Angels for six generations. He currently resides in the Highland Park neighborhood of Los Angeles and is active in the community's visual and literary arts.

Susan Rogers considers poetry a vehicle for light and positive energy. She is a practitioner of Sukyo Mahikari—a spiritual practice promoting positive thoughts, words, and action (www.sukyomahikari.org). Her poems are included in numerous anthologies and journals, including *The Best Poems of San Diego, Pirene's Fountain,* and *Saint Julian's Press.* She was nominated for a Pushcart Prize in Poetry and was interviewed by Lois P. Jones for KPFK's *Poet's Café.*

Scott Rubenstein is a poet, teacher, and scholar of the heart. He has sold over 30 TV scripts, and was on staff for "Star Trek: The Next Generation." His short won Best Short at Moondance Film Festival and a documentary about humor and healing was nominated for a Peabody Award. A featured consultant on "The Daily Show," Scott is a sought-after speaker/teacher at universities and writing conferences, including USC, Columbia College West, CSUN, Hampshire College, and Tubingen University. He was included in the Penguin Anthology's *Now Write: Speculative Fiction*, with "Surprise in the 24th Century." He and his wife of 23 years wrote a poem on their first date and date every Tuesday doing improv with Aretha Sills.

Taura Scott reads and writes tanka at her home in sunny Pasadena, CA. Her work can be found in *Atlas Poetica, Ribbons, red lights, Moonbathing,* and other publications. She is a long-time member of Poets on Site and the Caltech Red Door poets.

Elsa M. J. Seifert, M.A., is an interfaith Spiritual Director and long-time resident of Altadena. After raising three sons, managing a business, and editing a Southern California newspaper, she now spends much of her time volunteering for nonprofits and writing essays, short stories, and poetry. Her work has appeared in *Altadena Poetry Review Anthology 2015, 2016, and 2017*; in *The Courage to Write* (Falcon Creek Books, 2011); *Authors in our Midst*, ebook, 2013; and *Poetry and Cookies Anthology* in the years 2011-2014. Her prose has appeared in the *Southern California Nevada News*, 1998-2008 (an insert of the national United Church of Christ News) and in *Hometown Pasadena*, an online newspaper.

Pamela Shea, Sunland-Tujunga's ninth Poet Laureate, is a writer and poet who chronicles her life through verse. She finds inspiration in family and nature as well as in triumph and strife. Photography has also become a recent passion for her. She was a featured reader and workshop leader at the Shouting Coyote Performing Festival, and has since participated in many readings with the Wide Open Readers, led by Elsa Frausto, and the Village Poets of Sunland-Tujunga at Bolton Hall. She has an extensive record of community service and has been employed in the medical and fitness fields.

Nancy Shiffrin is the author of two collections of poetry, *The Vast Unknowing* (Infinity Publishing), and *Game With Variations* (Unibook.com). The poems here are from *Flight*, a new chapbook. Nancy's prose is now collected on lulu.com. Visit her at http://home.earthlink.net

Dorothy Skiles served with the County of Los Angeles, Department of Public Social Services for over 34 years. She was named Poet Laureate of Sunland-Tujunga, 2012-2014. Since 2010, Dorothy has been a member of the Village Poets of Sunland-Tujunga. She has published four chapbooks, two of which were in collaboration with fellow poets. Her poems are in *Meditation on Divine Names* (Moonrise Press, 2012), and *From Benicia With Love* (Accent Digital Publishing, 2013). In July 2015, she was featured in *Colorado Boulevard.net* in Pasadena, "Mapping the Artist: Dorothy Skiles." Her poems also appeared in the *Altadena Poetry Review Anthology 2016* and the *Altadena Poetry Review Anthology 2017*. Dorothy is also a member of P.E.O. (Philanthropic Educational Organization), Chapter KU, that promotes educational opportunities for women.

E. Russell Smith retired from teaching many years ago to devote his full time to investigative journalism and other writing. He now divides his life between

Pasadena, CA and Ottawa, ON, Canada. He has published two novels, a collection of short stories, and four volumes of poetry. His poetry reflects variously on natural phenomena, civil life (Canadian and American), and progressive religion.

Robert Stewart is his own patron supporting his studio through the printing industry since the sixties until he was replaced by computers in 2000. He is happiest being in his studio ever since. Poetry comes naturally by working alone on his creations for hours. One's mind thinks of things easy and pointed.

Mary Langer Thompson, Ph.D., has had articles, short stories, and poetry appear in various journals and anthologies. She is a contributor to *The Working Poet* (Autumn House Press) and *Women in Poetry: Tips on Writing, Teaching and Publishing by Successful Women Poets* (McFarland). She was the 2012 Senior Poet Laureate of California. A retired school principal and English teacher, she now writes full time.

Mary E. Torregrossa is a *story-listener*, a practice honed by her job as an ESL teacher in Southern California. Originally from Rhode Island, Mary blends experiences from both coasts into her poetry. Her poetry has appeared in *Bearing the Mask: Southwestern Persona Poems*; in *Wide Awake: Poets of Los Angeles and Beyond*; and in *Voices From Leimert Park Redux,* in addition to numerous local anthologies and literary journals.

Maja Trochimczyk, Ph.D., is a Polish American poet, music historian, photographer, and author of six books on music, most recently *Frédéric Chopin: A Research and Information Guide* (rev. ed., 2015). Trochimczyk's seven books of poetry include *Rose Always, Miriam's Iris, Slicing the Bread, Into Light, The Rainy Bread,* and two anthologies, *Chopin with Cherries* and *Meditations on Divine Names*. A former Poet Laureate of Sunland-Tujunga, she is the founder of Moonrise Press, and Board Secretary of the Polish American Historical Association. Hundreds of her poems, studies, articles, and chapters have appeared in English and in translations. She is a recipient of awards from the American Council of Learned Societies, Polish Ministry of Culture, Polish American Historical Association, McGill University, and USC. Her website is www.trochimczyk.net

Jane Vander Velde is a Pasadena teacher and writer who moved to the area after living for 50 years in the Midwest. She was astonished by the exotic flora and fauna here, and delighted that the children at her school, Weizmann Day

School, coexist peacefully with peacocks, iguanas, and hummingbirds on a daily basis. Jane and her husband enjoy traveling in Southern California, as well as throughout the U.S. and Europe. Jane is looking forward to retirement in the next few years so she can see her three children more often and spend more time painting, traveling, and writing.

Alicia Viguer-Espert is a Mediterranean woman from Valencia, Spain, as well as an Angeleno. She's the winner of the San Gabriel Valley Poetry Festival Broadside Contest 2017and the San Gabriel Valley Poetry Festival Book Contest of 2017. Her work has appeared in *Lummox, Statement Magazine, Spectrum,* and the 2017 *ZZyZx Writer Z Anthology Intersections.*

Claudine Voznick is a working mother with a passion for art, writing and gardening. Her degree from Mt. St. Mary's College is in Liberal Studies with a concentration in Literature. Her love of poetry started in high school with a fascination for the English poets, Alfred Lord Tennyson, T.S. Eliot, and Elizabeth Barrett Browning. While these poets still and will always hold a special place in her heart, she has become more aware and appreciative of "our own", such as Frank O'Hara, Anne Sexton, and Mary Oliver. She feels that poetry is the answer to most of the unrequited questions of her heart.

Lori Wall-Holloway, a wife, mother and proud grandmother of nine grandchildren, lives in the San Gabriel Valley, where her poetry has appeared in the *San Gabriel Valley Poetry Quarterlies, Poetry and Cookies Anthology,* and the *Altadena Poetry Review Anthology* in 2015, 2016, and 2017. Her work has also been published in the *Spectrum Anthologies.*

Greg Ware has been an educator/administrator in California's San Gabriel Valley for the last 17 years. He has a Master's Degree in education and a teaching credential from Nova Southeastern University in Florida. In addition to nurturing young minds, Greg is an accomplished musician and producer with a Billboard Top 40 hit to his credit, along with over 20 songs featured on television. His poems are designed to enlighten and entertain, as there's more than one way to peel a parable. Yet the fruits of knowledge ripen in the highest branches, rarely harvested. Greg is also the Amazon Best-Selling author of the sci-fi inspirational thriller entitled, *Just Love Everybody.* This is an interactive novel with an accompanying CD of the same title, as the author showcases his musicality.

Jacquelyn Bellard Wilson is a retired educator of 40 years: preschool, elementary, and university levels. Her philosophy on teaching is that, to excel as a teacher, one must be open to and be guided by, intense learning. Wilson has been in love with words from a young age, writing poetry since age seven. Her poetry reflects her observations and reflections of the world in love, social commentary, and growth. Her words speak to self-awareness, understanding, resolution, and determination to experience life passionately and with compassion. Her poetry has been published in the *Altadena Poetry Review Anthology 2015* and *2016*.

Kath Abela Wilson is the leader of Pasadena's Poets on Site poetry writing and performance group, meeting three times a week near Caltech. With her husband Rick, mathematician and historical flute player, she travels internationally to math, music, and poetry conferences. She writes a weekly poetry column for the online magazine *ColoradoBlvd.net*. Her chapbooks, *Driftwood Monster* and *The Owl Still Asking*, were recently published in the Locofo Chaps series, Moria Press, Chicago, from Lulu.com. Kath Abela publishes in many journals and anthologies. Her social media presence is Kathabela Wilson on Facebook and @kathabela on Twitter.

Joe Witt resides in Altadena, CA with his wife Roz, and their two cats, ShadieLadie and Mouse. They have one son, two grandsons, and two step-grandchildren, who keep them busy. Retired from JPL in 2002, Joe is currently learning to kiteboard. He is in Mira Mataric's creative writing class at the Pasadena Senior Center and has had a tanka, a haiku, and a poem published.

J.K. Won has lived in Southern California most of his life. He primarily writes short-form poetry. He participates in poetry readings in the local area, and his poetry has been published in a few journals.

Annette Wong is a poet, part-time lawyer, podcast host, and career consultant who lives in Los Angeles. She is a member of the Pasadena Rose Poets and a regular at Elline Lipkin's Writing Workshops Los Angeles poetry class.

Helen Yagake has lived in Pasadena since the age of five, when her family left Japan to settle in the United States. She has been interested in creative writing since junior high school and was first published in John Muir's poetry review in 1969.